PENGUIN BOOKS

Wednesday's Child

Shane Dunphy worked in child protection in south-east Ireland for fifteen years. He now tutors on childcare courses in Waterford City. He lives in Wexford with his wife and two children. *Wednesday's Child* is his first book.

Wednesday's Child

SHANE DUNPHY

PENGUIN BOOKS

PENGUIN BOOKS

Published by the Penguin Group

Penguin Ireland, 25 St Stephen's Green, Dublin 2, Ireland
(a division of Penguin Books Ltd)

Penguin Books Ltd, 80 Strand, London WC2R ORL, England

Penguin Group (USA) Inc., 375 Hudson Street, New York, New York 10014, USA

Penguin Group (Canada), 90 Eglinton Avenue East, Suite 700, Toronto, Ontario, Canada M4P 2Y3
(a division of Pearson Penguin Canada Inc.)

Penguin Group (Australia), 250 Camberwell Road, Camberwell, Victoria 3124, Australia
(a division of Pearson Australia Group Pty Ltd)

Penguin Books India Pvt Ltd, 11 Community Centre, Panchsheel Park, New Delhi – 110 017, India

Penguin Group (NZ), 67 Apollo Drive, Mairangi Bay, Auckland 1310, New Zealand
(a division of Pearson New Zealand Ltd)

Penguin Books (South Africa) (Pty) Ltd, 24 Sturdee Avenue, Rosebank, Johannesburg 2196, South Africa

Penguin Books Ltd, Registered Offices: 80 Strand, London WC2R ORL, England

www.penguin.com

First published by Gill & Macmillan Ltd 2006
Published in Penguin Books 2007

1

Copyright © Shane Dunphy, 2006
All rights reserved

The moral right of the author has been asserted

Set in 11.75/14 pt Monotype Garamond
Typeset by Rowland Phototypesetting Ltd, Bury St Edmunds, Suffolk
Printed in England by Clays Ltd, St Ives plc

ISBN: 978-1-844-88141-3

Monday's child is fair of face.
Tuesday's child is full of grace.
Wednesday's child is full of woe.
Thursday's child has far to go.
Friday's child is loving and giving.
Saturday's child works hard for a living.
But the child that is born on the Sabbath Day
Is bonnie and blithe and good and gay.

Children's Folk Rhyme

Contents

Preface

This book began life as a series of case studies for a doctoral thesis, and only very gradually, through the prompting and encouragement of others, became the story that you have before you today. It is a record of my experiences with three special families. It is not told as entertainment, but to show that in a society that is often insular and unwilling to look upon harsh realities, courageous struggles are going on daily, often unacknowledged, fought by those who dwell on the peripheries of our world.

I have been involved in social-care for more than fifteen years, and this book involves experiences taken from right across that time-span. For ease of reading, I have compressed the narrative into a single time-line. You will read the story of one year in the life of a child-protection worker, based in an office somewhere in Ireland, during a period in which what we now call the Health Executives were called the Health Boards. In reality these cases did not happen concurrently and could have occurred at any time across that fifteen-year period. To protect the identities of the children, adults and professionals involved all geographic details, family specifics, names and sometimes gender have been altered. All experiences did, however, happen.

In *Wednesday's Child* I discuss a number of other professionals I worked with. These are mostly composite characters, amalgamations of workers I have known and had the pleasure to work alongside. I have learned from everyone I have shared an office with, and I have tried to demonstrate that here.

I have reproduced procedure as well as I can recall it. If you notice any errors, they are all my own. Different regions operate different methods, and if the book reflects that, so be it.

PART ONE

First Week Blues

I went down to the town with my work boots on.
Man said: 'We got some work right here,
For those that got a mind, my son.'
Well I worked until my hands was raw
And my back was aching, stiff and sore.
Man said: 'Them's the first week blues,
And, son, it just gets worse from here!'

'The First Week Blues', traditional blues song

I

The day had started off badly. Thinking about it, I should have seen the signs, but back then I was dangerously optimistic. It is a character flaw that I have since corrected. I had arrived at the offices of the Child Protection Department at 10.30 a.m., and had immediately been taken to see Joe Strand, a social worker. Joe was a tall, fat man from Cork. It was my first day working on the team, so I didn't know Joe at all, but I could see that he was running a fever and was very ill. His breath rattled in and out of his well-padded chest and he was bathed in a sheen of sweat. He told me that a call had come in several minutes earlier to say that there was a disturbance out at the Kelly house in Doonan. He thought we should go out immediately, and asked me would I mind driving – he wasn't sure he was able.

I had been assigned my caseload only an hour before that and therefore had had no time to acclimatise myself to the various children and families I was representing. The file on the Kellys was vast, and I couldn't even remember the names of the four children in the family. I did know that they had the capacity to be extremely challenging and that a disturbance could only mean that we were heading into a potentially violent situation. As we walked to the car, Joe told me that the gardaí would be meeting us at the house, but that they wanted us to go in first to try and evaluate the situation. They had indicated that Mrs Kelly was in the house, along with at least two of the older kids, one of whom had an infant. The nature of the disturbance was still uncertain.

We drove through the town. It was a sunny morning, and early shoppers were going about their business. I tried to gather my thoughts. My caseload was made up of twelve cases, which ranged from multi-agency families like the Kellys to children in residential care who were at risk of their placements breaking down, to a couple of children in foster care who were proving to be problematic to their foster parents, and finally to the running of a group for children who were exhibiting challenging behaviour in school.

As I drove past the Church of the Sacred Heart on the main street, a mother and her small son, a curly-headed toddler, were standing at the curb waiting to cross. I was chatting inanely to Joe. To be honest, I was beginning to worry about him. He seemed to be drifting in and out of consciousness, and did not seem to be really aware at times of what was going on. I attempted to keep my tone light, but I was also trying to keep him with me. As we were about to drive past the gate of the church, the toddler slipped his hand out of his mother's and shot out into the line of traffic.

It's strange how things seem to slow down when a crisis occurs. I recollect seeing the child's face break into a wide, innocent grin. I remember him jumping in a loping, clumsy manner off the curb of the footpath, and almost losing balance as he hit the tarmac of the road. I saw the mother bringing her now empty hand to her mouth as she started to scream at the escaping child – interestingly, she didn't run after him. The child's frame crossed as if in slow motion in front of my car. I roared a profanity and hit the brakes as hard as I could.

I have very mixed views on religion. You don't remain in my line of work without coming to think that there's something out there, although you start to believe that it's not always altogether good. However, on this sunny morning, as I headed for an appointment with leering, capering insanity, somebody was watching out for me. The bonnet of my car stopped within centimetres of the toddler who, oblivious to the danger, continued to run awkwardly across the street. The mother was still standing on the footpath, watching the small figure of her child disappear into the crowd of pedestrians on the opposite side of the road.

'Would you ever watch out for your child?'

Joe had rolled down his window and was shouting at the shocked woman. Somehow, he had returned to consciousness for a few brief moments and had caught the near death of the adventurous toddler. His dulcet southern tones seemed to shake her out of her lethargy, and she suddenly broke into a run, crossing in front of us. I watched her go, and then returned pressure to the accelerator and moved forward.

'Jesus, that was a fuckin' close one,' I said, wiping the sweat from my brow.

'Lucky you weren't going a few miles an hour faster.' Joe was leaning his head against the head-rest and closing his eyes. Within moments he was gone again.

Doonan is a small village. It looks like something you would expect to see in *The Quiet Man*, surrounded by green fields, with white-washed thatched cottages here and there and pubs with names like the Horse and Hound. It is, however, a bad place. We would never visit there without letting the people back at the office know where we were, and we would never go alone. Two minimum.

The estate where the Kellys lived was up a short hill, past a small local shop. It had a horseshoe shape and was made up of fifteen houses, built in the late 1980s by the local County Council. Every single family in these houses had a social worker assigned to them. Some, like the Kellys, had more than one. It was almost a badge of honour.

I parked the car outside number eight, the Kelly homestead. I parked it pointing toward the exit of the estate, in case we needed to make a fast escape. Before we got out of the car, I rang the gardaí on my mobile phone, to tell them we had arrived and that we would call them if we needed backup. This was normal practice for a visit involving two agencies. They were parked two hundred yards up the road, they informed us, and were ready. I looked at Joe. He was completely unconscious, his head lying at a peculiar angle, his mouth wide open, a rivulet of saliva trickling down his chin. His breath smelt of illness, and sweat ran down his face in large droplets. I wondered for the hundredth time why he had come into work that morning. I nudged him in the chest with a finger.

'Joe, we're here.'

He stirred painfully and sat up, the hair on the back of his head matted and tangled.

'Okay, boy. Let's see what the story with this crowd is.'

He moved to open the door.

'Listen Joe,' I said, catching his arm. 'Are you up for this?'

He looked at me in surprise, his wide, bloodshot eyes a sharp contrast against the pallor of his skin.

'Oh aye,' he said, heaving himself out of the car.

The estate looked like something from a war-zone. Two gardens had burnt-out cars outside them. One house had a front window boarded up. There were several children playing out on the small, sparse green, all of them with the blank, desensitised look of the abandoned. The houses themselves were three-bedroomed bungalows, built box-like with the pebble-dashed walls that all local-authority houses of the period seem to have. As we moved around the car towards the open gateway to the house, the group of children gathered around us at a safe distance. I noted two small boys, both blond, with the familial likeness of brothers. They were dressed in threadbare tee-shirts and ill-matching shorts, and were filthy. With them was a little girl with dark pigtails and a red gash down the side of her left cheek. She looked to be about five years old, and had with her a child of indeterminate gender who was barely out of infancy, and who observed us with slack-jawed speculation, a black finger jammed up its right nostril and a slime of drool covering its chin.

I dragged my attention back to number eight as the sound of unintelligible shouting came from within, the garbled words being screamed by a hoarse, deep-voiced woman. Joe stumbled against me, his breath ragged gasps now. He muttered something I could not hear. I wasn't interested in trying to decipher his ramblings any more. There were more immediate concerns at hand.

As we approached the front door, it was opened by the largest woman I had ever seen. She stood around 5' 11", a good half-inch taller than me, and just slightly shorter than Joe, but it was her girth that was the most striking. I was stocky, but she dwarfed me, and she had incredibly muscular arms and shoulders. She was wearing a grey tee-shirt and a shapeless tartan skirt. But what was most frightening about her was her face. She exuded a kind of insane rage and her eyes blazed with an unquenchable hatred for real and imagined slights visited upon her by the world in general. Her hair was a mess of grey and black and it sat on the top of her huge head in a topography of knots and tangles that seemed to mirror her inner turmoil perfectly. I put her age at mid-fifties, but she could have been anything from forty to seventy. I realised that I had stopped in my tracks and was simply staring at her. Joe was slumped onto my shoulder again.

'What?' she bellowed, her whole body clenching with the force of the scream, her biceps bulging. 'What do yiz want here? Get the fuck away from my house!'

I was speechless. I was suddenly aware that Joe had raised his head and was looking at her with half-lidded eyes.

'Hello, Mrs Kelly. We heard there was a bit of a row goin' on. We wondered could we help at all?'

She glowered back at him. He had a half-smile on his round face, which dripped with perspiration from the strain.

'Could we . . .' he had to catch his breath, 'could we come in for a wee while, Mrs Kelly? Just to talk, like?'

She grunted and stepped back inside the darkness of the hallway.

The first thing that hit me was the stench. The house reeked of stale cooking fat, cigarette smoke and shit. The hallway was so gloomy that I couldn't make out much beyond a pile of what looked like old clothes against the wall. The hall was in an L-shape, and there were five doors leading off it. The woman pushed open the first door to the left, and we moved into the living room. The room was a simple rectangle, with a bare floor covered in tiles of a colour totally obscured by dirt. There was an ancient suite of furniture around the periphery of the room which had probably once been beige but was now a dirty brown. A large and new-looking television was in the corner, and the glowing embers of a fire were in the hearth. The fireplace itself was covered in about an inch of dust and ash, and was cracked and broken. In one of the armchairs sat a young woman with flaming red hair, smoking. An overflowing ashtray was balanced on the arm of the chair, and her gaze was focused on the television, which was showing *Richard and Judy* in a peculiar, orange tinge. Beside the young woman was a baby's pram. Mrs Kelly pushed me from behind and I staggered towards the couch. She deposited herself on the armchair in front of me and fumbled for a cigarette from a box of Majors.

'Mrs Kelly, my name is Shane Dunphy. I'm a community childcare worker and I've been assigned to your family. I'm here to help in any way I can.'

She struck a match and set fire to the tip of the cigarette. She grinned at me, which was almost more frightening than her previous fury.

'I don't think you can help me at all, young fella.'

'You seem very upset.'

She laughed, billowing smoke in great clouds over me.

'Well let me tell you this then, you little fuckin' bollix. I need to pay me electric bill or they're goin' to cut us off. I need to pay me gas bill, or they're goin' to cut that off. I need to buy coal for the fire and I need to buy food for the table. Can you reach into your fat-arse pocket and help me now, Mr Fuckin' Health Board?'

I cleared my throat and looked at Joe, who was apparently asleep beside me. He muttered something and shifted restlessly.

'I'm not here to offer that kind of help, Mrs Kelly. But I can give you some advice on how to get some help. The community welfare officer—'

She was on her feet and nose to nose with me so fast I didn't even see her move.

'I fuckin' spoke to the community welfare officer yesterday mornin', you stupid fucker! He said he can't help us any more! He says that a month or so with no electric will do us no harm! He says that every time the bills come in we get in trouble!'

Her breath reeked of tobacco, sour milk and bile. As she shouted, her spittle rained on me like bitter hail. I blinked and tried not to seem as scared as I was.

'Will ye shut the fuck up? I'm watchin' this,' the woman in the corner called at us. I heard another match being struck as she lit a cigarette. I glanced at her for an instant before turning my attention back to the clear and present danger in front of me, who was now growling like a rabid dog and frothing round the edges of her mouth. I smiled weakly at her and moved back slowly on the couch. Joe was stirring again beside me.

'Maybe we should just try and stay calm. Maybe I could ring the community welfare officer on your behalf, explain the situation . . .'

She turned back to her armchair. The cigarette in her hand had burnt down to the butt. I looked over at the redhead.

'I'm sorry, I didn't get your name.'

'That's cos I didn't tell you it,' she snapped, never taking her eyes off the screen.

'It's Geraldine.' Joe was with me again.

'Geraldine, I'm pleased to meet you. Is that your baby?'

She nodded.

'May I have a look?'

I stood up. Joe slid down into a half-lying position without my support, and stayed there. I moved over to the pram, keeping half an eye on the bulk that was now shaking and frothing. I looked into the pram. A baby of maybe three months was lying on a stained sheet, half-covered with a ragged shawl. It was awake and looked at me with large blue eyes. It had been sick, and white semi-digested milk lumps were dried on to the side of its face.

'Boy or a girl?' I asked.

'What?'

'Is your baby a boy or girl?'

'A girl. Christine.'

'May I?'

An indiscriminate shrug met my request, so I lifted the child out of the pram and went back to the couch, where I had to perch on the edge so as not to sit on Joe. The child continued to look at me. It gurgled and waved its chubby arms and kicked its legs. It was wearing a grey sleep suit which had probably started out life white, but which was black at the elbows and bum. I could tell that the nappy was full.

'I think she's due a change, Geraldine. I'll do it if you like. Don't get up.'

She hadn't moved or even registered my statement. The changing bag was beside the pram and I grabbed it and pulled it towards me. I found a semi-clean towel on the top of the bag and spread it out on the couch, shoving Joe's head aside to make room. Christine had a very slight nappy rash, but nothing too bad, and I quickly cleaned her and put on a fresh nappy. The nappies were a decent, named brand, as were the wipes and cream. I washed the puke off her face and freshened her up with the wipes: behind the ears and under the arms, her legs and feet. She seemed well fed and not unhappy. I sat her on my knee and looked back at Mrs Kelly, who was now rocking and swearing quietly.

'How long has your mother been like this, Geraldine?'

The redhead sighed and used the remote control to mute the television.

'She went mad last night. The ESB bill came. We've no money. She can't stand the stress.'

I nodded and gave Christine my index finger. She grasped it firmly and pulled at it. Reflexes seemed to be present and correct.

'There're a few of you living in the house here, aren't there? The youngest is fourteen, right? She's the only one at school. Can't you all club in and help her? Even if you aren't working, you've got the dole or Lone Parents or whatever . . .'

She was looking at me with real anger.

'You people make me fucking sick. You think you know it all, coming here in your big car, telling us how to live our lives. I don't have the money for the bill. The others don't have it either.'

I looked back at her unwaveringly.

'How much is the electricity bill?'

'It's not just one bill. There's the gas as well.'

'Okay. Bills. How much do you owe?'

A roar broke off my line of thought as Mrs Kelly thundered from the room. The door that she had wrenched open slammed off the wall, puncturing a hole in it that crumbled plaster all over the already grimy floor.

'I'd say it's about four hundred euro now.'

'For two bills?'

'We owe for the last ones too.'

I nodded. The cycle of poverty. I stroked the

baby's head and watched as she tried to focus her big eyes on my hand.

'If you could even pay something off them, they'd make allowances. They don't actually *want* to cut you off. Give them something to work with.'

She fumbled for another cigarette.

'Yeah, well fuck you.' She mumbled around the filter.

'Geraldine, come on! I'm trying to help you here. I'll ring them if you want, see if we can't work this out.'

She was shaking with rage and her cheeks were flushed with the embarrassment of the conversation. I could tell that she wasn't stupid, and that she had a sense of pride that simply did not belong in this slum. It would be knocked out of her the hard way. It was a wonder it hadn't been knocked out already.

'Whatever. I don't care any more.'

With a thunderous roar Mrs Kelly lumbered back into the living room, this time brandishing a bread-knife.

'Oh shit,' I muttered.

She was glaring at me with a savage intensity, her left hand bunched into a fist, her right hand clamped around the handle of the knife. I looked quickly at the blade. It was slightly rusted and far from razor sharp, but it would be enough to do some damage with her obviously manic strength behind it.

'Now you big bastard!' she seethed through clenched teeth and a constricted throat. 'You will listen to me!'

She drew the jagged end of the blade over her arm in a swooping arc, grating the flesh rather than cutting it. She grunted and did it again. The blood came immediately, running in thin sheets down her forearm.

'Mrs Kelly! Please!'

I quickly placed the baby back in the pram. She didn't make a sound, unaccustomed to being hastily dropped. I sat back down. I didn't want to threaten the woman by standing. She growled deep in her throat, and stood there, seemingly for a second unaware of what she was doing, where she was, even of my presence. Geraldine had gone back to her television. She looked mildly upset by the turn of events, but not so much as to lose track of the morning programme. Mrs Kelly slowly drew the blade over the flesh just above her wrist. I watched, my mind working rapidly. She was purposely not hitting the artery. She wasn't trying to kill herself – yet. I shot a lightning glance at Joe, but he was still out of it. The woman before me was growling again, and continuing to make red, raw grooves in her arm. I could hear the sound of the drops spattering on the floor and pulled my legs away from them.

'This isn't helping anyone, Mrs Kelly,' I said, barely aware of a tremble in my voice.

'You'll listen now, you bastard,' she said, her eyes fixed on me, trying to gauge my reaction.

'I was listening anyway!' I shot back, feeling desperate.

She blinked at that, uncertain.

'I was just chatting to Geraldine here, and we were saying how, if we could get ye all to club in together and pay a bit off each of the bills, it'll keep the services switched on. Weren't we, Geraldine?'

The redhead looked over at me in disgust, but nodded and grunted assent. The knife remained poised over the seeping arm.

'Could I have the knife, Mrs Kelly?' Joe asked, sitting up shakily.

He had his hand outstretched towards the huge woman, who was also trembling, the tears welling up in her eyes. She slowly placed the knife in his hand and sank down on the floor amidst the cigarette butts, the dust and the old newspapers and sobbed, rocking rhythmically. Joe sagged on the couch, panting, the knife blade held away from himself. I stood up and walked over to Geraldine, squatting down in front of her so that I was in her line of vision, obscuring *Richard and Judy*. There were tears streaming down her cheeks, although she wasn't making a sound. I took the smouldering cigarette from her and had a long drag on it. I hadn't smoked seriously in years, but suddenly needed one badly. I held her hand gently.

'I need to ring Dr Maloney to have your mam admitted as soon as possible. Today.'

She nodded, crying more openly now.

'I'll organise with the ESB and with Bord Gáis to have the bills paid in instalments, but you need to get your brother and sister to help with it. Can you do that?'

She nodded again. Mrs Kelly had begun to sing 'Mary Had a Little Lamb' as she rocked. She sounded like a little girl.

'You have a beautiful baby, Geraldine. She needs to be safe and this isn't a place for a child. You know that – maybe better than anyone.'

She nodded again. I pulled on the cigarette and flicked it into the fireplace. I stood up.

'I'm going to make a phone call. Will you be okay to watch your mother till I come back?'

Again a nod, this time accompanied by a sniff. I went over to Joe and grabbed his arm, hoisting him up. He came to consciousness as I lifted him and half-walked and was half-carried to the door. I dumped him in the passenger seat of the car and called the gardaí, asking for the squad car to come around, then called the office of Mrs Kelly's psychiatrist.

It took another two hours for her to be taken away. She remained locked in that childhood place all the time. Geraldine returned to sullenness, embarrassed by the vulnerability she had shown and the agreement that she should not be raising her child in the horror she herself had been raised in. I stood out by my car in that strange, tormented housing estate as the ambulance pulled away. The gardaí had taken Joe home and I was alone. I smoked a cigarette provided by one of the ambulance men and felt empty and tainted. Short of having a sick woman placed in hospital, had I achieved anything; had I helped in any sense at all? I sat into my car and started the engine. As I drove out of Doonan, the only thing that I knew was that there are sometimes situations in social care where there are truly no winners. And the day was only halfway through.

2

I ate lunch in a small café. I didn't know anyone in the office well enough to meet them for lunch, and anyway, I felt the need to be alone, to regroup my resources before my afternoon appointments. I had returned to fieldwork after two years of teaching college, training childcare workers, because I felt that I was getting out of touch with the work at the coal-face. I thought that I would benefit from reimmersing myself in the day-to-day realities of child-protection work. After a morning at the sharp end of it, I was already wondering if I had done the right thing. Was I really able for this after so long? What did I hope to achieve? Could I get the teaching post back if I prostrated myself before the Head of the Faculty? I pushed such thoughts aside and pulled myself together. I'd give it the week and then consider the best approach – outright begging, threats or simple bribery.

I paid for the meal and walked the short distance back to the office. Rosalind, the office administrator, was still at lunch when I came into the lobby, and I walked through and up the stairs to the work area. Downstairs was made up of Rosalind's office, a meeting room, an observation room and a playroom.

There were eight rooms upstairs, a small office for the team leader, a kitchen, a bathroom and five larger offices for the rest of the team. The rooms were all small and cramped, most with only one phone for often three or four people. I was based in the room at the top of the stairs. I had my diary open and was flicking through it as I came in the door of the room, but a voice stopped me in my tracks.

'Hi Shane.'

I looked up and saw a slim woman sitting in my chair. I looked at her blankly.

Her name was Melanie, and she was a social worker. She was, in fact, one of the reasons I was there, as she and several other workers were being moved to other projects.

And she was seated in my chair at my desk.

She was a talented worker and, from what I had gathered in the few brief conversations with members of the team before my arrival, had established herself squarely as a powerful matriarchal figure. She had subsequently been offered the job of setting up and managing a new team in a nearby village. This meant that she had a whole building at her disposal from which to work. She seemed, however, to feel the need to retain claim over her desk. I looked aghast at my small collection of stuff – a jam-jar full of pens, a notebook with phone numbers in it, a hardback ledger in which I logged phone calls – a collection that had been shoved aside to make room for a large pile of files and loose papers.

'You didn't think I was giving up my desk, did you?' she asked, smiling condescendingly.

'Yes, I did actually,' I said, still frozen to the spot.

'Well, I need it,' she retorted, pulling over the phone and punching in a number aggressively.

I stood and watched her, unsure what to do. Around the same age as myself (late twenties), she was slim and striking. She dressed like she had put a great deal of thought into it, and I would learn that her colours always matched and her accessories were always co-ordinated. Her dark hair was thick and worn shoulder length in an expensive cut.

She was fiercely territorial and I had been told, by her as well as by some of the other staff, that no one would ever fill her shoes. I was aware that she had a small group of followers among the social workers, and that there had been open aggression between her and the team-leader until this new post came up. It seemed that conflict was something that she did not go out of her way to avoid.

As she began her phone conversation, I reached over her and grabbed my stuff, pulling a chair up at a neighbouring desk. A numbness settled over me like a flame-proof blanket. To tell the truth, I was enraged. In this type of work, the office desk and small amount of miscellaneous junk are a person's base of operations and therefore sacrosanct. You don't screw with them. Although I was new to the team and new to the job, I still warranted this small amount of respect. Melanie, however, was an unknown quantity to me, and I knew enough to realise that she had the capacity – at the very least – to cause me a world of unwanted pain. I decided not to get into direct confrontation with her ... yet. There were political ramifications that were too complex for me to fully grasp. I would wait and see how best to handle her.

My afternoon appointments were all with the local Travellers' Centre, and I was getting up to leave when my mobile phone rang. The number that flashed up was our sister-office in a neighbouring village. I wasn't due to visit there until the following week, so was surprised to hear from them.

'Hello?'

'Shane Dunphy?'

'Speaking.'

'Hi. This is Mary Jeffries, Team Leader with the South Team.'

'Hi. What can I do for you? I don't think I'm due to meet you until next Wednesday.'

'No ... no you're not. It's just that an emergency has come up.'

She spoke with a broad Dublin accent in quick, short bursts. I could tell already that I would like her.

'An emergency?'

'Yes. Have you read the file on Gillian O'Gorman yet?'

'Barely at all.'

'Well, it seems she's had some sort of an episode at school. They need somebody to get out there.'

'Okay. I have some other meetings lined up, but

they're nothing that can't wait. Should I go alone? She's never met me before. If she's in an agitated state . . .'

'Is there anyone else there?'

I looked over at Melanie. The thoughts of going on a visit with her after the morning I'd had did not fill me with confidence. I heard a tread on the stair and Andi, the other Community Childcare Worker on the team, strolled in. Andi was a warm, friendly, open-faced girl who tended to dress in a slightly hippy style, all tie-dyes and paisley dresses and trousers. Her hair was long and curly and she always seemed to have a bounce in her step.

'Andi, are you free to do an emergency visit?' I called over.

'I can be.'

'Yeah,' back to the phone. 'Andi can come out with me.'

'Good stuff. Call me when you're done.'

I filled Andi in on what I had been told, which in fairness was virtually nothing, and waited while she cancelled her meetings. I used the phone in her office when she was finished (since Melanie was still talking loudly into the phone in mine) to make the single phone call required to cancel my own appointment, and we headed down to the car park.

'I'll drive,' Andi said as we left the building.

Andi drove a bright red Mini. We headed out of the town towards the village where Gillian O'Gorman went to school.

'I'm afraid that I don't know a whole lot about this kid,' I admitted.

Andi nodded, fiddling with the radio until she found a station playing traditional Irish music. She whistled along through her teeth, tapping the steering wheel in an off-beat rhythm.

'I play the bongo drum, y'know,' she said, looking at me from the corner of her eye.

I looked at her in bemusement. 'I didn't know that.'

She nodded again, battering the steering wheel some more and whistling without much tunefulness.

'I bet your neighbours love that. Not to mention any people who may be unfortunate enough to live with you.'

'Oh, Muriel doesn't mind. She plays the harmonica, so we get on fine.'

I had to laugh at the mental image of Andi (I imagined her house-mate as a similar hippy type) sitting up into the small wee hours of the morning playing terrible traditional music to one another and smoking joints made of home-grown hashish.

'Well that's nice. I'm glad you have each other to entertain. What do the respective boyfriends think of all the racket?'

She snorted through her nose.

'I don't have a boyfriend. I have Muriel. She's my life-partner.'

I nodded again.

'Good for you. Was it her harmonica playing that attracted you to her?'

She guffawed aloud at that, thumping me good-naturedly on the shoulder.

'Andi, as fascinated as I most certainly am at the concept of a pair of trad-loving, hippy musicians, I am meeting one of my clients in around ten minutes, and I'm at something of a loss. My only memory of her file is that it was fucking huge and that she has almost every imaginable problem. What exactly are we walking into out here?'

'Now that is a big question.' Andi pulled a pouch of tobacco out of a baggy pocket in her parka and tossed it into my lap. 'Roll me one of those.'

I proceeded to make her a roll-up, realising for the first time that I would be working with a gang of nicotine freaks. Andi had switched into professional mode and was giving me the edited highlights of the O'Gorman file.

'The O'Gormans have been known to the social work department for years. Libby, the mum, is a single parent, a manic-depressive and probably borderline schizophrenic. The dad disappeared years ago, and Libby won't talk about him. Sinéad, whom you'll meet (she's one of Melanie's clique), was the social worker on the case.'

I finished awkwardly rolling her the smoke and passed it over. She lit it from the dashboard lighter and continued, the cigarette dangling from her lips as she spoke.

'I have to hand it to Sinéad, she worked like hell with that family. She was out in the house with them day in and day out, and it looked like they were making some headway. But then, as always happens, Libby stopped allowing her entry. We were worried, so we went to the guards, and Gillian ended up being taken into care for a brief period. That was a disaster, because she kept running away. It wasn't a secure unit – they just didn't have the facilities to cope with her. Libby would be waiting for her in the town and they'd hitch to Dublin and book into a shelter there. This happened loads of times. It was a fucking joke. We couldn't stand over having anything to do with the case. We handed it to psychiatric services and pulled out. It nearly killed Sinéad.'

I sat there watching the countryside scroll by.

'And Gillian now?'

'Well, you're right, she's almost like an encyclopaedia of disorders. She's anorexic – I don't know how bad, I haven't seen her in months, but she had to be constantly watched when she was in the residential unit. She self-injures. She'll cut if there's a sharp implement available. If not, she'll fashion one out of tinfoil or a sharpened piece of wood. If that's not available, she'll throw herself downstairs, bounce off furniture, smash her head into the wall, pull out chunks of hair . . . whatever she can manage before she's restrained. She has been sexually abused on at least two occasions I know of – not familial abuse, that's at least one thing the family doesn't do to one another. She has a seriously warped relationship with her mother. It's almost like Gillian doesn't exist in and of herself; she's an extension of Libby. They actually occasionally speak in unison, like something off a TV horror movie. It's freaky.'

We were pulling into the schoolyard. Andi rolled down the window and tossed out the butt of the roll-up.

'I don't want to sound self-obsessed or gender fixated, but how is she with men? Has she been close to any outside the family?'

Andi was opening the door and getting out, reaching into the back and grabbing a shoulder bag.

'Not that I'm aware of. But then, she's never been particularly close with any women outside the family either. I think you're on as good a footing as I would be in similar circumstances.'

'At least she's met you before.'

'Yup. Frankly, I'm glad to be just along for the ride. Wouldn't be in your shoes for anything. You know you've got all the shit cases, don't you?'

I looked at her disconsolately as we walked toward the door of the school building.

'Have I?'

'Oh yeah. I actually asked for you to get one of mine. The McCoy kids? I think you're meeting them tomorrow. I gave you them.'

'Why?' I asked incredulously.

'Ooo . . . nasty case. Alcoholism, neglect, suicide . . . really shitty case. Nice kids though.'

'They're all nice kids!'

'No they're not. You know that as well as I do. We just tell ourselves that so we can do the job.'

'Well thanks for that, Andi.'

'Ah, no problem, babe.'

The school appeared to have been built some time around the 1900s. It was old, grey and crumbling, a long, three-storey rectangle with a tower reaching above it, attached to the end. The corridor was lined with paintings of nuns, landed gentry from the area and biblical figures, all looking sternly down on us as we followed the sign towards reception. Teenaged girls in purple uniforms – straight skirts, woollen knit jumpers, cream shirts and purple ties – passed us every now and again, the vacant glances of the hormonally besieged and dermatologically challenged assailing us on all sides. There was the ambient sound of the school all about us: the voices of the teachers raised above all else; the murmur of students; the scrape of chalk on the blackboard. We arrived at reception and told the mousy secretary who we were. She nodded and muttered something into the mouthpiece of an archaic-looking black phone.

'Sister Assumpta will be down to you in a moment. Would you take a seat please?' She spoke so quietly that I had to strain to hear her. We turned and moved to a row of chairs by the wall.

'These places always make me feel nervous,' Andi muttered.

'Catholic guilt?' I asked, glancing up the stairwell opposite us to see if the good Sister was on her way.

'Don't think so. I was raised neo-pagan. I just always get the impression that they're looking down on me or something when I'm in these kinds of schools. Like I should be apologising.'

'I believe that *is* Catholic guilt; you just don't know it yet. I think it's a latent Irish thing, whether you're actually Catholic or not. It's built into us all,' I told her as a tall, erect woman dressed in dark colours made her way down the stairs. 'Of course, if you really *are* pagan, you're damned lucky that you don't spontaneously burst into flames coming into a Catholic girls' school. Do you have 666 tattooed anywhere?'

'Shut up, you arsehole,' Andi retorted, glancing nervously up at the stained-glass window and moving out of a beam of rose-coloured light from one of the panes.

As she got closer, I saw that the tall woman had grey close-cropped hair and a face creased with laughter lines. I had to admit that she most certainly did not look as if she was about to preach at us about anything. She smiled broadly as she approached and I was struck by her height. She had to be at least six feet tall. She extended a hand to me.

'Welcome, welcome. I am Assumpta.'

'Dunphy. Shane.' I smiled back, standing and shaking the proffered hand, startled at first at the power of her shake. 'You know my colleague, Andi Murphy?'

'I do indeed. Welcome Miss Murphy. Well, I won't pretend that I'm not glad to see you both.' She was already moving back towards the stairs, her hand still on mine. She spoke in that quiet, purposefully gentle way that nuns seem to adopt. 'Our little Gillian is in something of a state, and I have become extremely concerned for her.'

'Could you tell us what happened, Sister?' Andi asked as we climbed the stairwell.

'Well, it blew up today because of a disagreement between Gillian and one of the other girls. Now, I don't blame Gillian at all. The other young lady is a known bully and has been trying to provoke Gillian for several weeks. I'm afraid she came off much the worse for it, though. Gillian has left claw-marks all down her face.'

I looked at Andi, who shrugged. If this was all we had been summoned for, it would be something of a waste of time. A child with a background like Gillian's was bound to have occasional episodes of aggression, especially if purposefully provoked, and, rightly or wrongly, I generally took it that a reasonably well-trained teacher should be able to deal with the odd physical outburst. It was an occupational hazard within the teaching profession.

'Was there anything else, Sister?' I asked.

She heaved a sigh and smiled, although her eyes when she turned them toward me were filled with sadness.

'There is much else. Maybe you should just see her.'

*

31

Sister Assumpta's office was at the top of the tower. It was a large, circular room that offered a view of the entire village and much of the land that lay around it. We waited while the nun went to get Gillian from class. She was gone a few minutes, and I was putting a book by Hemingway, *Islands in the Stream*, back on its shelf, marvelling that any nun could be a fan of the hard-drinking, sexually voracious adventurer (and then wondering why the hell not) when the door opened and Sister Assumpta came in, followed by a child. I had to do a double-take, because this child did not look fifteen. At first glance I would have taken her for ten. Then I realised what I was seeing. Andi was standing by the window. Her mouth hung open, but she had the sense to say nothing.

Sister Assumpta pulled out a chair for the child and looked over the back of it at us, the pain evident in her eyes. Gillian was in what must have been close to the final stages of anorexia nervosa before it became terminal. She weighed around 56 pounds and I wondered how much of that was oversized clothes and attitude. Her hair was thin and stringy. Her skin had achieved an almost transparent state such was its pallor. Her eyes were bloodshot and sunken in her head, twin pinpoints of anger, fear and paranoia. Her cheekbones jutted out of her face like blades and her shoulders were obvious precipices through her shirt and jumper. I could see all the bones of her knees clearly, and her shoes and socks had long since become too big for her.

'This is Gillian, Mr Dunphy,' Sister Assumpta said.

I looked down at the emaciated creature who also had me locked in a vice-like gaze. I realised as I looked more closely that the girl was shaking. I didn't know if it was from weakness or nerves. I glanced over at Andi for a moment, but saw that there were tears welling in her eyes. She turned back to face the window, and I was left momentarily the sole focus of my new client.

There are times when you have no time to think, when you just have to rely on training and instinct. I have long since realised that thinking by and large just gets me into trouble, so I've developed a kind of trip-switch in my head. It goes when I reach a point of over-load or when what I'm faced with is so dire that reason is just useless. The switch trips, power gets re-routed and I'm on pure auto-pilot. I let intuition take over and just trust that somewhere in my memory bank is an answer, a course of action that won't cause me to fuck up entirely.

This was – obviously – one of those occasions.

A number of stray thoughts flitted across my consciousness. Gillian was obviously scared. She couldn't have been more than five foot two, and was a frighteningly undernourished weight. She was an adolescent faced with a big, adult male with long hair and a beard whom she had just been told was to be her new childcare worker. I was also aware that anorexia, at this advanced stage, causes an effect in the individual similar to that of a sedative. It releases endorphins into the system that create a natural high. Endorphins are a bit like morphine. Gillian was probably in an altered state, and liable to respond to me in any number of ways – outright panic, unfettered joy or utter apathy. I also noted that she was seated while I was standing. The first thing I did was to adjust that. I squatted down on my haunches and stayed at the distance I was at.

'Hey, Gillian,' I said as gently as possible while trying desperately not to sound patronising. 'I'm Shane. I've been asked to work with you.'

She was sucking breath in and out rapidly. I was worried about hyperventilation. In her weakened state, I thought it was very likely. I needed to keep her calm and focused on me. I edged a microscopic bit closer and smiled at her gently.

'I'm here because the Sister was getting worried about you. Andi brought me out.' I nodded in the direction of Andi, who was turned back around to face us, her eyes red but clear.

The girl glanced briefly over at Andi, then shot her attention right back on to me.

'I hear you had a bit of a row today.'

No response.

'It's no big deal. You're not in trouble or anything. I hear that you were kind of pushed into it. Not that attacking someone is always the best way to deal with stuff, but sometimes we all lose the head.'

The same silent stare. The shakes were lessening. It seemed they *had* been caused by nerves. As I spoke, I infinitesimally edged forward.

'I think that what the Sister and the other teachers are most worried about, Gillian, is the fact that you maybe haven't been eating much lately.'

A slight reaction – a twitch of the lips – barely noticeable.

'Could we talk about that? I'm not gonna make you do anything you aren't comfortable with, and I know that right now, eating probably makes you feel very uncomfortable, but we need to talk about it, okay?'

She looked over at Andi again, then a quick glance over her shoulder at the Sister.

'I know that if I were to tell you that I was going to fix you up something to eat, and that I wanted you to eat it, it would make you feel sick to your stomach. It would be like I was trying to poison you. Does that sound about right?'

A ferocious nodding of the head. She was listening now.

'So right off, I am not going to try to make you eat today. We will have to get to that, but you need a little bit of help before we try it out. I'm here, and I know you won't believe this right away, but I'm here completely for you. My only job is to listen to what you have to say, and to make time for you and to try and help you to have it easier at home and at school and with any other part of your life you want to talk to me about.'

She looked puzzled at that statement. I doubted that anyone had ever stated the job description of

35

the community-childcare worker so baldly to her before. The truth is, there is no specific job description – it depends on the worker and the region, but as far as I could ever understand, that was it. You represent the child and are the specific liaison between the child and any other official agency they are in contact with.

'So, do you want to talk about how you're doing today? Andi and I came out because we heard you were having a tough time, and that maybe you needed some help. I'm here. Andi is here in case you felt a little scared talking to me, seeing as we never met before. Would you like it if I asked Sister Assumpta to just let us hang for a few minutes?'

A barely perceptible nod. But a nod for all that. I was in.

'Sister, could you leave me and Andi with Gillian? You can keep the door open and wait outside, but you see, my job is to be here just specially for Gillian, and I need her to tell me how I can help her right now. Would that be okay, Gillian?'

A small nod. More obvious this time. I know it may seem like I'd been wading through treacle with this girl, but this was actually alarmingly swift progress. I felt the tension begin to ease from me. I let emotion flood back in, and did a quick internal check of how I was doing. This was a trick I had developed while still a student. We tend to be very aware of how we are making the children we work with feel, how they are responding to us, but we often forget to examine how they are making *us* feel. As a human being, you need to constantly reflect on your own emotional landscape. I quickly did just that. It had been a tough day so far, but I was still more or less intact. I was struck by the child's courage, and knew that I was responding to it. She had been in a physical confrontation earlier in the day, an incident that must have exhausted her, and now she was being hassled by a stranger from the Health Board, an organisation that had probably caused her little more than grief in the past. It was remarkable that she was dealing with me at all. I was aghast at her physical condition, and was struck by a deep sense of anger that she had been neglected to the point that she was like this. I was also drawn to her eyes. There was a deep inner strength and a real humanity in those eyes. And a well of pain. She was hurting. It seeped from her like pus. I could feel it as an electrical pulse, this child's hurting.

Assumpta moved around the chair and out the door, which she left open. I heard a chair scraping the floorboards as it was pulled up outside. I stood, hearing my knees pop and slowly walked over to a chair by the wall, which I moved over to within a safe distance of Gillian. I nodded at Andi, who took a chair and moved to within a similar distance. At this proximity, I could see that Gillian had a fine growth of hair over her face and arms. This was a clear sign of advanced anorexia – it meant that she had lost her natural layer of body fat. The body

37

compensated by producing the coating of hair, to keep in warmth. I had only seen this once before, and that child had not survived. People often forget that anorexia, if left untreated, can be fatal.

'So, Gillian,' I said, trying to sound as upbeat as possible, 'how can I help?'

She looked away from both of us for a moment, suddenly embarrassed by the attention and putting on the precocious huff of adolescence. I smiled to see it. At least it was normal behaviour.

'I don't want a worker,' she said finally, her face flushing so much through the pallor, I was again worried she might pass out.

'Is it because I'm a guy?'

Again she looked away, gripping her sides tightly. Eventually she nodded, still not meeting my gaze.

'Well, I can understand that. If I were a girl, I probably wouldn't want me for a worker either. But you know, we'll get used to each other. And we don't have to rush into anything either. I mean, if you're worried I might be weird or something, we can meet outside the school and go for coffee or something, where there's lots of people around. You'd be completely safe. I'm not gonna try and get you to talk about anything deep or really personal or anything like that. Whatever you want to talk about is okay by me. It'll be your time. But there is one thing that I *do* have to ask you to do for me first. I'm gonna have to ask your mam to take you to see the doctor.'

She shot a glance at me that held a fair degree of venom.

'I'm *asking* you as your new worker, but I think you know that I can *make* you go if I wanted to. You look like you haven't eaten in a really long time, Gill, and you may need to take some medicine to help you to build up your strength again. You know, a tonic or something.'

She looked at her knees, her lower lip stuck out in a ferocious sulk.

'You seem pretty mad at me for saying that.'

'You people always lie!' she hissed.

'Why do you say that?'

'You tell me that we don't have to rush into anythin' and then you tell me that I have to go and see the doctor! And you tell me that Mammy will have to come and you don't know my mammy. She'll be mad and there'll be trouble. And she'll go mad when she knows that they have a man seein' me and you'll get it. She'll do you good!'

I tried not to look too bemused by this outburst.

'Gillian, I'm afraid that your health can't wait for us to get better acquainted. I wouldn't be a very good worker to you if I let you go on right now without a doctor having a look at you. I'm not going to ask you to eat today – I said I wouldn't – but you are very close to making yourself really sick. I don't mind you being mad at me. And I expect that your mum will be cross about me seeing you at first, even though I think that letters have been sent out to tell her that I'll be working with you, so she should know.'

'We don't always get letters because of the dogs.'

'Oh.'

I wasn't sure what that meant, but figured I'd get a chance to ask about it later.

She continued to sulk.

'One thing that I will never do, Gill, is lie. I'm telling you right now about the visit to the doctor because it has to happen, and pretending that it doesn't won't help anyone. So I'm telling you straight up. With me, there are only two rules. When you're with me, you don't hurt anyone, me and you included, and you try your best. I follow those rules, and I'll ask you to. Part of not hurting is no lies. Lies hurt, and I'm not into that. I reckon you've been lied to enough.'

She made a kind of snorting noise.

'So what happened today?'

'With Maggie?'

'Is that her name?'

'Yeah.'

'So. You want to tell me what happened?'

'Not really. She was makin' fun of me, so I did her. Did her good too.'

'So I hear. What was she saying to you?'

'Nothin'.'

'Must have been more than nothing for you to do her so good.'

'She was callin' me names and stuff.'

'Bad names, huh?'

A nod.

'She was sayin' that we're all mad. That my mammy lets the dogs ride her.'

I said nothing to that. There didn't seem a right thing to say.

'Them things aren't true. Them are bad things to say about a person's family.'

Gillian looked up at me, and all the fight had gone out of her.

'Will you take me home, please?'

It was as sudden and as immediate as that. It was as if her battery had run down. I figured that in fact that probably wasn't far from the truth: the outburst of the day, coupled with her anger at me for telling her of her imminent visit to the doctor had effectively used up all her reserves of energy. She had burnt herself out. She sat in the seat, her eyes glazed over, her shoulders hunched up. I called for Sister Assumpta and she got Gillian's coat and bag, and we walked her down to the car. She said not a word, and climbed into the back without protest. I turned to Sister Assumpta before getting in myself. I couldn't hide the anger in my eyes, and she stepped back a bit when she saw it.

'How could she be allowed to get to this stage, Sister? You'd better tell me that you've been calling and calling for help, because I'll chase this one up and someone will have to answer for it. You seem like a nice lady and this seems like a good school, but so help me if I find that she has been left to starve herself because she's the local redneck's kid and no one gives a good god-damn, I'll be coming back out here with the fucking inspector and a fucking warrant and we're going to have us a very, very close look at your child-protection policies and procedures. I'm not arrogant enough to believe that I can have the school closed down, but believe me, someone will lose their job.'

She nodded, and I knew from the expression on her face that if there was any fault here, it didn't lie with her.

'I have been ringing your offices on an almost weekly basis. You are the first person to come out in two months of calling.'

'I'll check that, Sister.'

'I would expect no less.'

I nodded at her, some of the anger dissipating.

'I'll see you soon.'

She turned and walked back into the school building.

'You strapped in, Gillian?' Andi asked as she started the engine.

No response. It was really as if the Gillian I had seen for that short outburst was gone, had fled deep inside. I glanced back, saw that she was safely harnessed and nodded at Andi. We pulled out of the schoolyard and turned out towards the Dublin road.

The O'Gorman homestead was a kind of shack set deep within many acres of farmland. It had to be accessed down a long dirt track with tall trees and overgrown ditches on both sides. The only sounds as we moved across the terrain was the cawing from the many rookeries dotted around the perimeters of the fields and the occasional burst from a song thrush coming from the ditches on either side of us. At one point a rickety wooden bridge had to be navigated, and I wondered if it would support our weight.

The Mini's arrival at the O'Gorman home was accompanied by the noise of furious barking and slavering from four dogs of indeterminate breed that were all tied up to dilapidated vehicles around the property. The front yard contained the remains of several old cars, and a pile of tattered couches towered over us near the front dry-stone wall. It was hard to tell how old the property was. It looked as if parts of it had been built at various points in the nineteenth century, but one section to the rear certainly seemed to be contemporary. While the dogs were unable to get beyond the perimeters of the O'Gorman demesne because of the chains to which they were attached, they had free rein within its confines. It meant that no one without a death wish could attempt to gain access. The animal closest to my window was rearing up on its hind legs and doing its utmost to reach me. It looked worryingly like a Rottweiler, although there appeared to be traces of Alsation in the mix as well. It was truly the ugliest and most vicious beast I had ever seen.

'I see what you mean about not getting the post,' I said.

Gillian was already climbing out.

'Could you ask your mum to come out and see me for a moment, Gillian?' I asked.

She ignored me totally, wandering among the snarling dogs as if they weren't there. The dogs for their part ignored her too. At one point she moved so close to one it collided with her as it leapt in the direction of the car, causing her to stagger, but the dog did not even so much as look at her, correcting itself and continuing to snarl and growl in our direction. She picked herself up and disappeared around the side of the house. Even to these animals, Gillian seemed barely worth a thought.

'I suppose we wait for her mum to come to us,' I said to Andi.

'You're the boss.'

We waited.

Half an hour later the dogs were still not tired of trying to get loose from their chains to devour us, and Gillian's mother had still not appeared.

'Well, any more bright ideas?' Andi asked.

'Let's wait a bit more.'

It was nearing four o'clock.

I knew what was going on. We were being tested. Both Gillian and her mother were aware we were out there – from the noise of the beasts they had to be. The test was: how long would we stay? I could be a stubborn bastard, and I had nothing better to do.

'What happened to you back at the school?' I asked Andi, not looking at her as I spoke.

I felt her shift uncomfortably in the seat.

'Sorry. I wasn't ready for how far she's gone. Sorry I left you in the lurch.'

'That's okay. I'm getting kind of used to it today.'

'Look in her file when you next get a chance. There are some photos of her . . . before.'

'What she said about what that girl – Maggie – said about her mother. I take it that they're just childish insults?'

Andi rolled a cigarette and offered me the pouch. I took it from her and began to roll one for myself.

'Well, the O'Gormans are the local shit-kickers, so it's kind of a normal insult in these rural areas to suggest that you're having relations with the livestock. But there have been stories.'

'That she's fucking one of the dogs?'

'Yup.'

'One of those dogs?'

'The one at the back of the house.'

I looked over at a beast that seemed to be mostly Labrador but with the pointed ears of a terrier. It was chained, just like the others, but there were also some boards nailed up to separate it from the rest of the animals. It was obviously considered different in some way, but I baulked at the notion that it was being kept for carnal reasons.

'Handsome beast.'

'Gorgeous.'

Five o'clock rolled around. Andi looked at me.

'I'm getting pissed off, Shane.'

'Well, do you want to call it a day?'

Andi leaned her whole weight on the car's horn. And stayed there. The horn was surprisingly loud. It, incredibly, silenced the dogs for a moment. They stood there in surprise, their tongues lolling out over yellow teeth. Then the barking erupted again in competition.

'Watch *Countdown* now, you bitch,' Andi muttered.

It took ten more minutes of barking and horn competing before the front door opened and a woman came out.

I put her in her early forties. She was dressed in faded jeans and a raggedy woollen jumper, and her brown hair looked as if it hadn't been washed in weeks. As soon as she set foot outside the door, the dogs became silent and stood quietly watching her. She approached us smiling, walking easily and in a relaxed manner, as if we hadn't been there for an hour and a half waiting for her to deign to speak to us.

'And here's the lady of the house,' Andi said, finally letting go of the horn.

As Libby O'Gorman got closer, I saw that she had once been extremely beautiful. Harsh circumstances had taken their toll, but the residue of how stunning she had been was still very much in evidence. As she came to stand outside my window and Andi pressed the button to lower the glass, I became aware of a powerful sexuality. She exuded it from every pore, and I could see how she had such a huge hold over her daughter and how she had proven such a problem for so many Health Board workers. There was a strong intellect at play here – albeit tempered by psychiatric problems of deep complexity. She smiled at me, and I smelled alcohol from her. Cheap whiskey.

'Well, I didn't know you were here at all,' she said. Her voice was husky and full of humour. We all knew she was lying. It was a game.

'That's okay, Mrs O'Gorman. We weren't in a hurry. It's a pleasant afternoon to be out of doors in the country. Those are some fine dogs you have.'

She looked appreciatively at the animals, now sitting and dozing in the late-afternoon light.

'They're grand, aren't they?'

I smiled and tried to steer the conversation to the subject of her daughter. I needed to introduce the concept of me as Gillian's new worker, and also instruct her to bring the child to the doctor for a checkup as soon as possible. I had to assert that, while I would try to work in partnership with her, I was, fortunately or unfortunately, in charge to a large degree. I had statutory power, and could have Gillian taken into care. This is a factor that is always underlying any interaction between a parent and a state-appointed child-protection worker. Since the development of the Child Care Act 1991, the Health Board and the gardaí have the power, if they feel that a child is at serious and immediate risk, to remove

47

that child without a warrant. This means, effectively, that at any moment, if I felt that Gillian was in danger, I could call for garda assistance and have Gillian placed in care without reference to the courts or anyone else. I would have to secure an Emergency Care Order within three days of this, but that would not be difficult under the circumstances. I always had a policy of not pulling rank with a parent unless it was necessary, but I had a sense that Libby was going to give me plenty of cause during our relationship.

'Mrs O'Gorman, my name is Shane Dunphy, and I've been appointed to work with Gillian for the next while. Did you receive any letters about that?'

She laughed aloud in a great guffaw.

'Do you think that any postman is going to want to bring letters out here? I pick up letters in the post office in town every now and again. It's usually nothing I would have wanted delivered anyway.'

She eyed me with suspicion and some interest. I wasn't sure quite what to make of her inspection. It seemed almost an invasion.

'They've sent you? That's a new approach, I'll give you that. She'll not want to work with you, Mister. You might as well just fuck off back where you came from.'

'I'd like the chance to try. I talked to her at her school today. She . . . talked back. It was a start.'

'She's a little flirt. She's like her mother.'

This was followed by a rolling of the eyes and a

licking of lips in a mock of sexuality that was just a little disturbing, as I could see Gillian very clearly in her.

'Mrs O'Gorman—'

'Call me Libby.'

'Thank you. Libby, Gillian is dangerously underweight. I don't know if you're aware, but she doesn't look like she's eaten in several weeks. Has she been eating meals at home?'

'Dunno. She sits down with me.'

'Is she vomiting it back up?' Andi piped up from beside me. 'Libby, we've talked to you about Gillian's anorexia before. She needs to be watched.'

'Ah, she's a wilful creature. I can't watch her all the time. She eats and then she pukes. She's been at that since she was a young one. I can't follow her into the toilet! What do you want me to do?'

'Follow her into the toilet,' I said quietly. 'When she's like this, you do what you have to, Libby.'

'Easy to see you're not a parent of a teenager, Mister. You try following a fifteen-year-old into the bathroom.'

'I have done so in the past.'

'You're full of shit, Mister.'

I let that one slide. There was nowhere to go with it that was productive.

'Libby, I want you to make an appointment to take Gillian to your GP. I need to have her looked over. When the weight of a person drops to the level she's

49

at it has fairly severe knock-on effects on the organs. She's putting herself at risk now, and she needs to be seen by a medic as soon as possible. I know you have a medical card – it'll cost you nothing. If transport is a problem, I can organise that also. But Libby, I will be checking to make sure she goes. I want you to go with her tomorrow.'

I knew that I had crossed a line with her. Her eyes narrowed and she stepped back from the window. Just like her daughter, she had shut down.

'Right,' she said, moving back towards the house, her eyes still fixed on me as she slowly paced backwards.

The dogs seemed to sense a change in mood, and the growling resumed as the beasts rose, their hackles up as if by some unspoken command. Then she was at the door of the house and was gone, and the air about us exploded into noise and ferocity again.

Andi turned the key in the ignition and we reversed back up the dirt path for half a mile until we could turn. We said nothing.

When we reached the main road she looked over at me, sunk in my seat and deep in thought.

'So what did you make of that, Mister?'

I smiled and looked over at her, mental and emotional exhaustion settling over me like a shroud. I couldn't remember the last time I had felt this way. It was like every drop of emotional resistance had been wrung from me. My brain felt like cotton wool.

'I don't know what to think.'

'Well you must have some comment. How do you think you're going to get on with them?'

'I think,' I said, struggling for anything useful to say, 'that I am in way over my head.'

Andi laughed aloud and patted me on the knee.

'Once you know that, Shane, you'll do fine.'

We drove through the beautiful midlands countryside as the sun dipped over the hills, and my first day of casework came to an end. As we headed back towards the office, I reflected on the fact that I had not achieved one single thing that day, other than probably alienating two sets of clients and the Principal of a local school. I reckoned that I could be thoroughly proud of myself.

'How d'you think I did?'

'You seemed to do grand so far as I could see. But then, I don't know shite.'

'Thanks.'

'Shane, go home, have some dinner, watch something mindless on the television and forget about it. There's tomorrow and the day after and the day after that etc., etc., etc. The O'Gormans and the Kellys and all the others you have on your caseload aren't going anywhere. You might be public enemy number one today, but in a week or three weeks the phone will ring and there will be Libby O'Gorman on the other end looking for you to do something for her, and you'll be the *man*. She's a manipulator. And Gillian is learning the same behaviour. She'll flutter her eyelashes and expect you to come running. You did the right thing today. You laid some solid ground rules about how your relationship will work. The trick with the O'Gormans is to stick by them.'

I knew she was right.

'You in a hurry to get home?'

'Not especially.'

'Let me buy you dinner?'

'I like Indian.'

'Indian's good. Muriel won't mind?'

'She works nights at the shelter. She won't be home until around midnight. Until then, I'm a free agent.'

'Well drive on then. I presume you know a good place.'

'Oh no. The Indian place in town is terrible. I said that I liked Indian. I didn't say the restaurant was any good.'

'Oh. Well, let's go somewhere else then.'

'No! I like Indian!'

'But I thought you said . . .'

'We will go to the Indian place and will put up with it! It might not be any good, but it's the only place in town.'

'I tell you what. Just as long as it doesn't give me food poisoning, I'll give it a shot.'

'Can't promise that.'

I looked over at her, and in the failing light I could see that she was barely suppressing a huge grin. I was glad of her company, and as we made our way back into town the ridiculous conversation continued and

Andi and I put the day behind us and effortlessly became friends. It was a friendship I would come to value a great deal over the next year and, when everything began to fall asunder, she would be there for me when few others were.

3

The next day dawned bright and cold.

I was renting a small cottage in a tiny hamlet about twenty miles from town, and was still very much living out of boxes. I had moved in on the Monday, started work on the Tuesday and was unpacking as I went along. The cottage consisted of two tiny bedrooms, a good-sized and quite cosy living room which had an open fire and an old (but very comfortable) suite of furniture, a shower and toilet, and a kitchen that was so small I reckoned that the previous occupants must have been the Seven Dwarves. I crawled out of bed, stumbled into the shower and, after I had scrubbed myself into an acceptable level of consciousness, made a pot of coffee. I had to dig around in a cardboard box and unwrap a clean cup from newspaper, only to find of course that I had to wash it anyway to get the newsprint off.

I munched on dry brown toast and drank the coffee as I read the paper, Miles Davis's *Kind of Blue* playing on a small stereo system I had unpacked. In my head I was going over the events of the previous day, wondering if I could have done things differently. Eventually I gave it up. Maybe I could have been more gentle with Sister Assumpta. But then, Gillian's state warranted the comments I made. Perhaps I could have handled the situation at the Kelly's better, calmed Mrs Kelly, been more sympathetic. I wondered whether I should have refused to go out ten minutes after arriving in the office for the first time with an obviously sick man. Maybe, maybe, maybe . . . social care is full of maybes. There are almost no absolutes. I checked my diary for the day. There was to be a staff meeting at ten, which would take most of the morning, and I was visiting the McCoys, the family Andi had kindly passed on to me, in the afternoon. Hoping it would be quieter than the previous day, I got in my car and headed for town.

The offices of the Social Work Department were the busiest I had yet seen them. The full complement of staff, twenty people in all, were in for the meeting. I made my way up to my office. No Melanie this time, but a load of papers and files that were obviously hers were strewn across the desk. I knew that I would not last the week without having a showdown with her over this, and pulled up a chair.

I reached over to my file cabinet and took out the O'Gorman file. To say that it was huge would be an understatement. I was not even going to begin to try and read it then. I planned to take home some of my bigger case files to read in my own time (this was frowned upon by management as a security risk, but it was fairly common practice) and for now just riffled through the paperwork, looking for something specific. Five minutes later I found what I was looking for. Four coloured Polaroid photographs of Gillian were among the reports and letters. They had obviously been taken while she was on a trip with a group of other children – possibly even when she was in residential care. They showed her horse-riding; at a table in a restaurant with an enormous pizza in front of her; hugging another girl as they stood outside a cinema, both of them grinning and making antennae with their fingers behind each others' heads; pulling on a bowling shoe and looking irritated at being photographed. The photos were similar to any you would see of a normal, happy teenage girl. What was jarring about them, and what had caused Andi to advise me to look them over, was the obvious change in Gillian. In these photos she was certainly slim, but she looked healthy and full-faced and pretty. The spindly, hollow-eyed creature I had met the day before was almost unrecognisable as the child in these photographs. I looked at them for a long time.

Photographs do not always tell the truth. People perform for the camera when they know it's on them, putting up a façade and hiding who they really are. The best photos are those taken when the subject is unaware. The photo I kept coming back to was the one of Gillian on horseback. In it she was hunched over the pony's neck, a riding helmet that was much too big for her head was pushed back on her forehead and she was looking to the side nervously. In the other three photographs you could mistake Gillian for a well-adjusted girl, full of fun. Not in this one.

That pain I had seen was present here in those brown eyes. She was looking at something off on the horizon line, something that seemed to be moving away from her, something she could not quite make out. I wondered if she had ever managed to capture it, whatever it was.

'Shane?'

The voice startled me. A tall woman, maybe thirty-five years old, with long, black hair stood at the door. She was dressed in a long, black dress and black, high-heeled boots with a white, crocheted cardigan loose over the outfit.

'Hi,' I said, realising that I had made my way through the assembled group without saying 'hello' to anyone and had come straight to my desk. I suddenly felt very rude and anti-social.

'I'm Josephine, Team Leader.'

She extended a hand, smiling. Yesterday she had been out sick.

'I'm sorry,' I began, standing up. 'I just wanted to check the file. I had no time yesterday and I had to go into a couple of cases fairly cold. I didn't mean to ignore everyone.'

She laughed, brushing away the apology. She was full of abundant good humour, shaking my hand vigorously and placing her other hand on my shoulder.

'Oh, don't worry, I understand. I heard that you had some fun yesterday morning all right. Baptism of fire, or what? You must think that we are the worst crowd going! I feel awful. I should have been here to meet you and make sure you settled in.'

'Not at all! You were ill. I got on fine. I was quite impressed with Joe, actually. He got that knife off Mrs Kelly while he was only really semi-conscious. Had to be seen to be believed!'

She laughed again, leaning back against the door frame.

'Will you join us in the kitchen for a coffee? There's a nice bakery just down the road and we get some scones and cakes delivered up on Wednesdays for the team meetings. Call it a hidden incentive. One of the few rules that I have is that everyone make every possible effort to attend the team meetings. I understand if you're in court or if there's a case conference you have to attend or an emergency visit you just *have* to make, but that shouldn't happen more than once or twice in a year. All the other weeks in the year, I want you here on a Wednesday morning.'

'Got you.'

'Good. Then we'll get along fine. Now, come and have coffee and an apple sponge and meet some of your new colleagues. You look like an apple-sponge man to me.'

'Well, I guess we'll see, won't we?'

She laughed again and led me out the door and across to the kitchen.

'Yes, we will.'

The meeting itself took place in the room downstairs. A circle of chairs was pulled up and the assembled throng, most still clutching mugs of tea or coffee, gathered round. Minutes of the previous meeting and an agenda for this one had been distributed into our pigeon holes that morning. They were about cases and issues that I had, as yet, no knowledge of. There was also a notice that training in Child Sexual Abuse Assessment was being made available in the coming month, but only to social workers. I felt the old irritation at this kind of slight.

The lines of rank and file among the professions are clearly drawn out in Social Care in Ireland. In other countries, I had learned, they were far looser, but in the class-conscious society that has developed here everyone must know their place and live with it. The order ran as follows: at the top of the pile are the social workers. They run the cases and must make all major decisions as to how a case is operated. In practice there are many cases that have no social worker, and there are indeed social workers with a great deal of respect for their non-social-work colleagues, but the fact remains that rank can be and is pulled on an all too regular basis.

Next in line are the childcare workers. Their role, as I have already stated, is to work in a therapeutic and child-centred way with their clients, representing them at case conferences and presenting their needs and opinions to any agencies they are working with. Childcare workers are much more 'at the coal-face' than social workers. Their contact with the children is more constant and more regular.

The final link in the chain are the family support workers. Their job is to work with families in an holistic way, assisting with matters such as financial management, behaviour management with challenging children, hygiene and nutrition.

The reason for this hierarchy stems, probably, from qualifications. In the past, social workers had degrees while childcare workers did not. Family support workers, despite the hugely important work they do, were rarely qualified, and often only worked part-time. While this is no longer the case, the delineation remains.

The meeting rattled on until 12.30 or so, and then everyone broke for lunch. Lunch happened in a pub just down the road from the offices. I stood at the bar, feeling uncomfortable, like a child on his first day at school. I ordered coffee and a club sandwich, and then found Andi at my arm, leading me to a table.

I remember reading an article in *Empire* magazine about the making of the movie *Planet of the Apes*. It observed that during breaks in filming, the actors playing the apes in the movie would automatically congregate in the canteen with actors who were wearing make-up of a similar breed of ape. So a visitor to the set would see a table full of gorillas, a table full of orang-utans, a table full of chimpanzees. No one forced this, it wasn't a 'method technique', it just naturally occurred.

In the pub this lunchtime, I found myself participating in something very similar. At the table Andi led me to were the two family support workers, Marjorie and Betty. Andi pushed me into a chair and sat down beside me. And there we sat: childcare workers and family support workers, the two lowest primate groupings on the Child Protection Team.

'So you're the new boy in class.' Marjorie smiled at me.

Marjorie was dressed in a long, tie-dyed skirt and beaded top with Doc Marten boots. Betty was very smartly dressed in a suede suit, a cigarette already smouldering in her hand and her eyes languidly half-closed.

'What in the name of God brings you to this godforsaken part of the universe?' she asked, blowing smoke out of the corner of her mouth.

'I'm a sucker for punishment,' I said, shaking my head at the proffered box of cigarettes.

'You must be.'

'You're not from around here,' Marjorie said, putting sugar into her coffee and helping me to move plates and ashtrays as our food arrived.

'No. I'm from Wexford. I have family here, though. That's how I know the area.'

'So you're not quite a blow-in.'

'Well, I've only really been here on visits before, so I'm hardly a local.'

'Well, you're very welcome anyway.' Betty grinned.

'Thanks. Any hints on survival?'

'With the cases you've been given?'

Marjorie and Betty shared a wry glance.

'Well, I reckon you've got two choices really,' Marjorie said, solemnly patting the back of my hand.

'And they are?'

'You can drown or you can thrash your arms about and scream for help.'

I raised an eyebrow.

'I don't follow.'

'I've seen people who were loaded with the real problem cases, who worked themselves ragged, never complained, never caused a fuss and who ended up actually quite poorly as a result of the stress. D'you see Melanie over there?'

She gesticulated with her head towards the person in question, who was sitting at a table on the other side of the pub with a group of cronies.

'Could I possibly miss her?'

'They tried to do it to her: gave her the worst cases, ran her ragged. And do you know what happened?'

I glanced in the direction of the subject of our discussion. Melanie's voice could be heard above the rest of the chatter in the pub, and her booming laugh punctuated our conversation like a depth charge.

'You know,' I said, 'she doesn't look like she's under too much strain.'

'That's because she just refused to continue with it. She threw a terrible strop, brought her case right to the childcare manager.'

In the Community Care Department within the Health Boards in Ireland, teams were led by team leaders, who are always social workers. All the teams are co-ordinated by the senior social worker. The senior social worker (as well as the heads of Disability Services, Residential Services and a range of other teams and providers) is answerable to the childcare manager, who was usually a social worker but was sometimes a therapist or psychologist, as our child-care manager was.

'Her caseload was cut right back. She wasn't popular for it, but they never took her for granted again.'

'That's good to know.'

'Now take her side-kick there. Sinéad.'

Sinéad was the social worker Andi had mentioned to me in relation to Gillian O'Gorman. Petite and gregarious, she was sitting with Melanie, and was almost as loud.

'Sinéad is a different story,' Betty chimed in. 'She arrived here practically straight from college. Full of enthusiasm she was. Wanted to save the world. No case was too tough for her, no working day was too long, no assistance was ever asked for. Every child and every family was a crusade.'

I said nothing in response to this description. I recognised some of the traits in myself and just shifted uncomfortably on the seat. I knew that these women were attempting to teach me something important, and suspected that Andi was behind it.

'They put her on the O'Gorman case and a couple of other real stinkers. It wasn't weight of numbers with her – it was the types of cases. Every case was severe: multiple problems, usually on the books for years, little hope of making any real change. But Sinéad, God love her, would not be told. Every day she'd arrive into the office and you'd just know that she was telling herself that today, today would be the day she'd make a difference to these children. And of course she'd go out to their houses, full of vim and vigour, and the children and their parents would be waiting for her with those dark, dark clouds hanging over their heads and all that baggage dragging along behind them, and she'd get drowned by the hopelessness of it day after day after day without fail.'

Andi, who had said nothing so far, joined the chorus.

'When the O'Gorman case fell apart, she fell apart too. It was just too much for her to bear. You see, Shane, we're supposed to be the good guys. Other people reject these kids, not us. But here was a case where we *did* reject the kids we were supposed to be representing, and Sinéad was the contact person, the face that they thought of when they thought of the Health Board. She had to take some time out; started seeing a therapist. All that noise, her being in with Melanie – it's just a front. She's hurting inside. I don't know how she keeps coming to work.'

I picked up a quarter of my as yet untouched sandwich. 'You three sure know how to make a bloke feel welcome,' I said. 'I appear to be on a rocky road to an inevitable breakdown.'

They laughed, but looked embarrassed. 'All we're

saying,' Betty said gently, 'is that in this type of work you have to be all things to all people – sometimes you feel like you don't even know who you are any more, you wear so many different masks during the average working day. You can go from being the "universal aunty" to the "avenging angel" in the space of an afternoon – sometimes you have to be both at the same time for Christ's sake! You can lose yourself very easily. There are a hell of a lot of skills needed to do what we do, but one of the most important is the ability to ask for help if you need it – *before* you hit rock bottom. We've all been there. I bet that even good ol' Melanie has been there too; that's why she wasn't prepared to end up in *that* place again. She may not be everyone's favourite person, but we could all learn something from her.'

I sipped my lukewarm coffee and smiled at the concerned faces.

'Remind me of that after my afternoon visit.'

'I will,' said Betty, lighting another smoke. 'I'm going with you.'

We were to pick up Victor McCoy from the small secondary school in the seaside village where he lived. I watched as the throng of children burst out of the gate, wondering if I would be able to pick Victor out from the crowd. Of course Betty knew him, but it's a game I sometimes play with myself. After years of working with, for want of a better word, 'troubled' children, I often find that I can pick a new client out of a gathering, or spy a potential challenge in a new class of children straight off. I identified Victor without any difficulty at all.

He stood apart from the other children, smaller than the majority of them and with a bent-over, loose posture. His bag, which seemed almost empty, sat at his feet on the tarmac of the yard. He had made no move to leave the confines of the playground and had not even strayed far from the front door of the school building. He was gazing off into space, seemingly unaware of his surroundings. I wondered if he was looking for cloud-shapes or observing birds in the trees beyond the perimeter line of the fence.

'I'll go and get him,' Betty said, opening the passenger door.

He was slouching against the wall, his left leg tangled with the strap of the schoolbag, his foot swinging, using the strap to create resistance, as if he was exercising the muscle. Betty was almost on top of him when he looked over at her. Had he noticed her coming and wanted her to make the effort to come to him, or was he oblivious of her approach? He certainly did not jump when she called to him, just moved his face around to look at her. I saw her lips move and she gestured with a nod toward the car. Victor's eyes moved in my direction. He slowly unfolded from the wall and moved to pick up the bag, only then noticing that it was still wrapped about his legs. He almost fell getting it but then followed

Betty to the car. I turned as he climbed in the back, extending my hand.

'Hey, Victor. I'm Shane. Good to meet you.'

My hand was taken in a loose, light grip, but not shaken. He did not meet my eyes, just looked at the floor of the car.

'We'll head straight home, Victor,' Betty said. 'I want Shane to meet your dad. We'll pick Cordelia and Ibar up at the house, and then maybe the five of us can go and get an ice-cream and have a chat.'

I thought I heard a muttered 'okay' from the back, but I couldn't be sure.

The McCoy house was a renovated cottage that may have once been a farm labourer's home or even a holiday chalet, not that I could imagine anyone holidaying in that barren little village. Victor got out silently and walked to the door. Betty gave me a look that said: we're in for a long afternoon. We followed the round-shouldered Victor up the short path. He was ringing the bell repeatedly and opening the letter box and calling through it in a hoarse voice – I got the impression that Victor was not used to speaking, and shouting seemed to cause him strain.

'What's the story, Victor?' I asked. 'Dad not home?'

He looked at me nervously for the first time, chewing his lower lip and scratching frantically behind his left ear. I kept my eyes on his and reached out and banged as hard as I could on the door.

'Maybe he just nodded off,' I said. 'Happens to me

sometimes. Big lunch, boring afternoon TV. Nothing to worry about.'

We listened to the silence that seemed to boom from the house.

'I bet he's just dropped out for milk or something,' Betty said, patting Victor on the shoulder (he cringed at the touch and she pulled back rapidly). 'Let's wait in the car.'

We got back in and I turned on a Top 40 station. I detest Top 40 radio, but I have found that most children and teenagers listen to it pathologically, so I have become immune. Betty rolled down the window and lit a cigarette.

'I'm sure he'll be back in a moment,' she said again.

Silence from the back.

An hour later a pretty blonde girl in a different school uniform to Victor's, who was leading a small boy by the hand, turned into the garden and knocked on the door. Before I knew what had happened, Victor was out of the car and beside them, talking quietly and urgently and throwing glances in our direction.

'Cordelia and Ibar, I presume?' I asked Betty.

'The very same.'

Cordelia said a few words to the now very anxious Victor and strode purposefully to the window through which Betty was smoking. Betty flicked the butt of her cigarette aside and smiled at the teenager. Ibar sat on the ground, all his attention focused on a beetle that had crawled from the grass verge. Close up, Cordelia was not just pretty; she was beautiful. I knew from the conversation Betty and I had earlier that she was thirteen years old – Victor was fourteen, Ibar six. She looked, however, a couple of years older than that and projected a sense of control and maturity that made you immediately sit up and take notice. This was a young woman who knew what she wanted and would do what had to be done to get it. I could tell who was in charge in this family.

The background to the McCoy case was simple and straightforward. This was something of a relief after the complicated cases I had encountered the day before. Victor, Cordelia and Ibar lived in the cottage with their father, Max, who was an alcoholic in recent recovery. The family was English. The children's mother, Beatrice, had died from an accidental overdose when Ibar was six months old. There had been talk that the death had been suicide. The reports from English Social Services, with whom we had a reasonably good relationship, suggested that there had been some domestic violence, although it appeared to be on both sides, with Beatrice giving as good as she got.

At any rate, the investigating detectives declared the death self-inflicted. Max moved from one unskilled job to another over the next few years, none of them lasting very long and many ending in his being asked to leave as alcohol began to take an ever more secure grip. Finally, as if fleeing something, Max and the children moved lock, stock and barrel across the Irish Sea and settled in the village. Max secured a job as caretaker of the local school and his drinking went from bad to terrible. The family was befriended by some of the locals, particularly the parish priest and a couple of women who worked as cleaners in the school and the church. It was through these people that the McCoys came to the attention of the Social Work Department.

This informal support network felt that the children were being sorely neglected, with Cordelia playing the role of wife and mother to the three males. Max was barely functioning in his job at the school, and Victor was regressing further and further into himself. Ibar exhibited extremely aggressive behaviour in the junior infants class he attended. What brought matters to a head was Cordelia turning up to one of Victor's parent-teacher meetings. The teacher in question did not know how to respond to this child with the eyes of an adult sitting before him, with Victor's report card clutched in her hand and a list of perfectly reasonable questions about his academic development written out neatly on a piece of pink stationery. Social Services had been called in. Max was immediately sent to a clinic to dry out. The children were placed temporarily in the care of one of the local women who cleaned the church. Betty had been asked to visit them on a fairly casual basis during their brief foster placement, and she had also been checking on Max after his release from the clinic, helping him to deal with his new-found sobriety and with his role as both father and mother to these children. My role was, primarily, to do some work with Victor, who, it had been noticed by everyone in contact with him, was becoming more and more isolated. I could already see that there was genuine cause for worry.

Cordelia glared into my car at Betty, who, to her credit, smiled back beatifically.

'What are you doing here? You weren't supposed to be visiting today.'

'Well, we were just in the neighbourhood and thought we'd drop by. This is Shane Dunphy. He'll be doing some work with you and Victor.'

I nodded and smiled, trying to look confident but probably looking more sheepish than anything else. Cordelia was making me feel like an intruder, and I had to remind myself that *I* was supposed to be the responsible adult in this interaction.

'Well, it's not convenient this afternoon. Daddy has been called away and has asked me to take Victor and Ibar out for some tea. You'll have to come back another time.'

Her accent was peculiar. There were definite traces of an English accent, but there was also an American flavour and some very Irish aspects too. She spoke quickly, however, and with total confidence, as if she expected to be listened to and obeyed immediately, so that it was difficult to focus on her accent or locution.

Betty seemed momentarily fazed. Cordelia kept

her full focus on Betty during this brief lull. I realised that she had not looked at me at all. It seemed that she perceived Betty as being the one in charge and that, as the hired help, I did not warrant any attention. The pause continued and seemed to stretch out interminably. I was about to intercede when Betty said: 'Where has Max gone?'

'He's gone into town.'

'The bus will be due back in a few minutes. He'll surely be on it, seeing as you're home from school. We'll hang on and then we can all go and get something to eat together. Hop in.'

Cordelia stayed exactly where she was, although she seemed to have lost much of her bluster. It was obvious that she had no idea where her father was, and that his absence was as much news to her as it had been to Victor. Both these children were scared (Ibar, who was poking the beetle with his forefinger, seemed totally oblivious), and in their different ways were trying to hide it. I wondered what had been going on in that little cottage. Cordelia sagged in almost exactly the same manner as her brother, and suddenly she looked every bit her thirteen years. She opened the door, steered Ibar in first and then climbed into the back, Victor following. Glancing into the rear-view mirror I saw a look pass between them. I couldn't read what it meant, but it seemed to me to be a sigh of resignation.

We drove back into the village and I parked across the road from the bus stop.

'The bus from town gets in at half past four, doesn't it?' Betty asked.

Nods answered her question.

'Only a couple of minutes to wait then.'

The bus was only ten minutes late, and when it stopped three people disembarked.

None of them was Max McCoy.

I looked over at Betty. The atmosphere in the car had become tense. Betty and I knew the children were trying to keep whatever game was being played going, and they knew that we could clearly see that something was wrong. I started the engine.

'I'm going to drive back out to the house,' I said. 'I think that when we get there, we'll talk again about what's really going on.'

Cordelia started to speak. I cut across her before she could get the first word out. I had sat back for long enough.

'I'd like you to just think about things for now, Cordelia,' I said, keeping my tone level but firm. 'You've already spun us one yarn this afternoon, and I want to hear the truth from now on. We've done it your way. Now it's time for you to do it our way. Okay?'

I saw her eyes glaring at me in the rear-view mirror. She was barely keeping the anger in check, but then I reckoned that Cordelia was very good at keeping things in check. She had had a lot of practice.

When we were back out at the McCoy cottage, I killed the engine and turned to the children. Victor

73

was simply staring at his hands, his body slouched as low as it could go in the seat. He seemed to be trying to make himself as small as possible, sinking into the fabric of the car, seeking to disappear. Cordelia was looking straight ahead, past me and down the road as if looking for an escape route. Betty sighed deeply. Ibar was still silent and implacable.

'So what's going on?' I asked.

'You don't know where Max is, do you?' Betty said.

Victor began to mutter something unintelligible. Cordelia said: 'He should be here. But sometimes he . . . isn't. Just lately he's not been well.'

'He's been sick?' I asked.

'Yes. But not like the flu.'

'Has he been drinking again?' Betty asked, the pitch of her voice prompting me to place a hand on her arm. I knew why she was angry: she had invested a lot in this family, but by venting at the children she would only aggravate an already difficult situation. Besides, she would be shooting the messenger.

'A bit. But he's been down a lot too.' Cordelia seemed to have decided to come clean. 'Sometimes I think he'll hurt himself. I've tried to get him to talk, but he won't always talk, even to me. I've been worried. We've been worried.'

She put her arm around Victor, who in turn embraced Ibar, who looked at him as if he were mad and shrugged off the overture. I tried to think what to do. Max would probably show up in an hour or so, but in what condition? It struck me that his regular absences were, more than likely, times he had gone on a bender. His arrival would probably be an intoxicated one. I knew from experience and from my training that trying to talk to or reason with a man in the throes of drunkenness was an utter waste of time and energy. Of course Max may have just gone into town and missed the bus, but that was unlikely. The crux of the matter was that we had three minors in our care who, to all intents and purposes, had been abandoned. There was only one thing to do.

'Betty, would you ring the office and tell them what's happened?'

'Will do.'

'Do either of you two have a key?'

'No,' Cordelia said.

'I can get in,' Victor said quietly.

He raised his head and I realised that my initial diagnosis of him was all wrong. He was not intellectually disabled, or even slow. I saw a keen intellect, and suddenly a smile illuminated his face and he was no longer the slack-jawed pre-adolescent who had been with us all afternoon.

'When he doesn't come home, I get in through the back, and then I let Cordy and Ibar in. If I didn't do that, we'd be stuck outside until he gets back.'

'Can you show me?' I asked.

'Yes.'

He led me around the side of the house. The grass was unkempt and the back yard was overgrown with moss and was treacherous. He pointed at a small top window that led into what must have been the kitchen.

'There.'

'You can get in there?'

'Yes.'

'Okay then. Here.'

I made a step by cupping my hands together. He put his foot into it and I lifted him up so that he could grip the rim of the window. It opened easily – the latch was obviously broken. He gave me that mischievous smile again and then he was through, wriggling into the narrow space as if he were a snake. I waited a second and then the back door was opened. He motioned for me to come in.

Inside the house was gloomy in the early evening light. The kitchen was neat and tidy, though sparsely furnished. The linolcum was faded but appeared to have been recently washed. Victor was moving ahead of me through the shadows. I followed him, and found him standing in the door of the living room. I saw what he was looking at and, without thinking, placed my hand on his shoulder. He didn't flinch this time.

A man I took to be Max McCoy was sprawled half on, half off the couch. The curtains had been drawn, so the room was in darkness, but I could see the almost empty bottle of cheap vodka on the floor near his hand and the puddle of vomit congealing into the carpet. The stench in the room was appalling and I had to take shallow breaths for fear of gagging.

'He does this sometimes,' Victor said, his voice little more than a whisper. 'I think he does it because he's sad. I think he gets lonely for Mummy. I do, and I don't even remember her all that well.'

'Has he been doing it a lot, Victor? Have you and Cordelia and Ibar been left to look after yourselves a lot?'

'Cordy looks after us. She looks after Daddy most of the time too. Daddy says we'd be lost without her.'

'Mmm. Well, Cordelia needs to be looked after as well, you know. She's only a kid herself.'

'I know.' I heard the words catch as he fought to keep tears at bay and I squeezed his shoulder.

I walked over, opened the curtains and the window to let in the air. I then walked over to Max McCoy and shook him, gently at first but progressively harder. Eventually he started and looked at me through fuggy eyes. He was probably in his early forties with short salt-and-pepper hair and several days' growth of beard. He was dressed in ill-fitting jeans and a check shirt.

'Mr McCoy.' I said it louder than I needed to, but I wanted him to understand me clearly, or at least as clearly as he could in his present condition. 'Mr McCoy, I am a community childcare worker with the Health Board. I need to take Cordelia, Victor and Ibar into care this evening. You are not in a condition

77

to look after them. I'll be back out tomorrow to talk to you some more, when you're sober. Do you understand?'

'Y . . . yes . . . yes . . .'

Victor was still standing at the door. A loud banging announced Cordelia's desire to gain access. I had forgotten that she, Ibar and Betty were still outside. Max seemed to be trying to reclaim dominion over himself, but he was fighting a losing battle. I heard Victor opening the front door, and then Cordelia pushed past me and embraced her father, crying quietly. He looked at me with such shame and self-disgust, I had to look away. Ibar shot past us down the hall to one of the rooms, like an animal into a bolt-hole. Betty was standing beside Victor and motioned with her head for me to step outside. I followed her out to the front step. Victor lingered just inside the porch, watching Cordelia and his father, seemingly sensing that he was not required.

'There's a woman out by the coast road who will take them tonight. She had them when he was in getting dried out before.'

I nodded. 'It doesn't look like he stayed dry for long.'

Betty said nothing, fumbling for a cigarette with shaking hands. I took the box from her and tapped out a cigarette, lighting it for her. There were tears in her eyes and she wiped them away, taking the cigarette and inhaling deeply.

'I should have seen this coming. I was supposed

to be the contact worker! How could I have been so stupid?'

'You know how manipulative drunks can be. And those three have been colluding with him. Cordelia looks like she would be a very daunting adversary. You saw what they wanted you to see. The only reason we caught it now is because we called unannounced. It was pure chance.'

'It doesn't excuse the fact that I fucked up, and fucked up badly.'

'I can't absolve you of that, Betty. You'll just have to beat yourself up for a while over it. But of course, you know as well as I do that there's nothing to be gained by torturing yourself. Learn from it. Be more vigilant next time. You know what, though?'

'What?'

'There probably isn't a damn thing you could have done differently. He would have slipped up eventually, or he wouldn't. We caught him. The kids will be cared for this evening, and we'll come out here tomorrow and see what we can do. That is what is important.'

She sniffed and smiled at me. I gave her a quick hug and went into the living room. Max and Cordelia were on the couch. The tears had subsided, but both were still hiccoughing and sighing. It seemed that Max had come to himself a bit in the few moments.

'I'm Max McCoy,' he said.

'Shane Dunphy.' I offered my hand but he made no move to take it.

'I am not pleased with myself, Mr Dunphy. I know what I am, and what I am doing to my children.'

'I'm not here to judge you, Mr McCoy. My role is to represent the children. You understand that I must remove them, for this evening at the very least.'

He nodded. Cordelia wrapped her arms around him even more tightly.

'I'll come out to see you tomorrow morning and we'll discuss how to proceed from here. It strikes me that you may need some more therapy to help you deal with the addiction, but that isn't my decision to make.'

'Oh, it's not, eh?'

'No. I will have a social worker accompanying me to discuss those issues with you. As I said, my role is to be here for the children.'

'We don't need you!' Cordelia spat at me then with such vehemence I almost stepped back. 'We're doing fine. Daddy just needs to get better, that's all. I can help him. We can fix this together, as a family.'

Max smiled in a tired kind of way and stroked his daughter's hair gently, hushing her as she disintegrated into tears again, less controlled this time.

'There are things that are too big for anyone to do on their own, Cordelia,' I said. 'Your dad needs some help from people who are trained to give it to him. You've done your best, but you're a child. You shouldn't have to cope with all this on your own. You need someone to help you, to mind you. That's what I'm here for, until your dad is in better shape.

I know you love him, and I can see that he loves you, but, as you said, he's not well right now.'

Max continued to hush the crying girl. Victor stood by the wall, apparently examining the pattern on the wallpaper, blocking out the horrors that were enfolding about him. Ibar was still nowhere to be seen. I doubted that he knew what was going on – but he knew something was up. Betty led Victor back into the hallway, suggesting that he gather some things for an overnight stay, and went to look for the younger boy. I wandered back out into the yard and watched the sun begin to sink below the hills across the road from the cottage.

We left them in the care of a woman named Dympna Dunleavey. She was not what I expected. I had foreseen a frumpy, spinsterish woman with blue-rinse hair. Dympna was probably thirty-two with short, dark brown hair and a pretty, friendly face. I felt at ease leaving the children with her; she seemed a warm, gentle person. Cordelia seemed, to my relief, to be fond of her, hugging her tightly as soon as we arrived. Ibar went to her for a brief cuddle and then disappeared into the house, first giving me a look that I could not read.

Dympna made us coffee and when the children had gone to their respective rooms she talked a little about Max, and how he was doing.

'I've been waiting for this to happen,' she said. 'He's been going down now for weeks. I don't think he was ever sober at all, to tell the truth. He was seen in the pub a week after he came back from drying out.'

'Why didn't anyone tell us?' Betty asked, incredulous.

'Sure weren't the social workers already working with him? You couldn't be called in when you were already there!'

I winced, knowing how those words would hurt Betty.

'Dympna, if this . . . er . . . placement . . . needs to be for more than one night, would you be agreeable? We will, of course, organise the full maintenance allowance for you immediately.' Foster parents receive a small payment for each child they care for, which, while better than nothing, is really just a token. No one gets into fostering for the money.

'Well, I can take the kids for a few weeks if it's really necessary, but I wouldn't really like to have them for much longer than that. I have other commitments.'

'Of course. We appreciate your being able to help us at all.'

I thought that we could get Max cleaned up within a few weeks and that we would not need a foster placement for any longer than that. Once again, I was allowing optimism to get in the way of reality. Little did I know it, but this case would test me and my personal resources in ways I could never have imagined. As I sat and drank coffee and the night slowly fell upon us, I thought that we had staved off disaster for the McCoys. For this family, I thought, there will be better days.

I could not have been more wrong.

4

I was the first to arrive at the McCoy house the next morning, and I parked up the road a bit and finished writing my report on the previous day's events while I waited. Shortly, I saw Noreen, a social worker who had worked on the case before, pull in and I got out and went over to her car.

'What happened?' she asked, abandoning any preamble.

I told her.

'Shit. I thought he was clean. We put a lot of effort into this guy.'

I shrugged. What did she want me to say?

'Where's Betty?'

'On her way I presume.' I felt myself begin to bristle. This was not my fault. I had not placed the alcohol in Max McCoy's hand, and I had not created the policy that said that a social worker needed to sign off on a Voluntary Care Order. I had not appointed Noreen to the case, either.

I pushed the rising anger aside. I was tired and contrary. It was likely that Noreen had either had to cancel or postpone something else to be there, and she probably wanted this finished as soon as possible so that she could get on with her day. Social workers have extremely heavy caseloads, and Noreen was no exception. I saw Betty's car turn into the road.

Max McCoy opened the door, looking as if he had spent the previous night on survival manoeuvres with the SAS. He stood aside to allow us into his hallway. He had obviously been cleaning, for the smell of disinfectant and polish lingered in a rather unpleasant cocktail in the air. But it was better than the smell of vomit. He silently walked into the living room, leaving us standing in the hall. After some seconds of looking uncomfortably at one another, Noreen followed him, and we trailed after her. He was sitting on the same couch I had found him on the day before, staring into space, his stubbled chin cradled in his hand, his hair sticking up at odd angles. He had rings under his eyes and I could smell his breath from the doorway. It was foul, but the alcohol in it was only a memory.

'Let's get this over with,' he said.

Noreen sat on the arm of one of the chairs and began to riffle through her bag.

'Your children are fine, Max,' Betty said, going over and sitting down beside him. 'I dropped in on Dympna on the way over this morning. She brought them to school and they're in good form. They're asking after you and looking forward to coming home.'

He heaved a deep sigh.

'Thank you, Betty.'

Noreen produced the Care Order and handed it to him.

'This is a similar Order to the previous one you signed. Do you need me to explain any of it to you again?'

'No.'

I handed him my pen, and he looked at me right in the eye. I was almost bowled over by the depth of misery I saw in him. I saw loss, shame, anger, bitterness and a terrible awareness that this was a battle he would never, ever be able to win. I saw, in that second, the story of Max McCoy from his own perspective. I saw his own abandonment, his own deep-rooted fear. I saw the little boy he had once been who had never received the love and support he deserved and needed. I saw an infant who had cried in the darkness and cried and cried, but no one ever came. I saw how handing his own children over to the authorities for a second time was driving another nail into the coffin that was his life. I wanted to reach out then and tell him to stop, to shout at him not to sign the paper; we would find some way to work it out. But I knew that this was not my place, and that the child he had once been was dead and gone. There were three other children who needed to be helped, and by signing this Order he *was* helping them, terrible though the cost was.

He signed the paper and pushed it across the table to Noreen, who countersigned it.

'What now?' he asked, looking around at us.

'Well, that's kind of up to you, Max,' I said, leaning

against the wall and folding my arms. 'What happened? I'm told by these two ladies that you were sent to a centre to get you cleaned up. You were released with glowing reports, you seemed ready to get on with your life, and then . . . this. What went wrong?'

'Oh God, Shane,' he said, rubbing his eyes with his knuckles and shaking his head, 'what kind of a question is that? Do you have any idea? Do you have a clue, man?' His tone was very defensive.

I was tempted to soften my approach, but I felt that being gentle would not serve him well now.

'I think that it's the only question to ask right now, Max. I had to stand here while your children watched you wipe puke from your chin and drag yourself out of a drunken stupor, and then I had to come back out here this morning to have you sign them away for a second time. That makes me feel pretty crappy, to tell you the truth. I think my question is a fairly reasonable one.'

'Aw Jesus. I don't know . . . things got on top of me. I thought I could cope and then . . . then I couldn't, you know?' His tone changed to whining, pleading, pathetic now. The aggression hadn't worked. He was trying a different tack.

'How do we know that it won't happen again?' Betty asked. 'How do we know that this isn't just another lapse in a long line of lapses? Those children won't be able to cope with this again. Look at what you're doing to them.'

'I know, I know. I feel awful. The kids mean everything to me. They're all I have. I need this sorted out. I have to get them back.'

'Are you serious about that, Max? Do you really mean it this time?' Noreen asked. 'If you are, we'll help in any way we can. We'll organise regular access visits, we'll get you specialist addiction counselling, we'll make sure that the kids get plenty of help too, but we need to know that you are committed to the process.'

'Of course I am. I don't know what happened. I don't know how I slipped back into the drinking. One minute I'm sober and steady, the next I'm coming out of a three-day jag. I don't know.'

'Do you have any liquor in the house now, Max?' I asked.

'No. I poured it all down the lav this morning.'

'Are you sure? If I were to do a thorough search would I find any in the toilet cistern or hidden in one of those cushion covers?'

'Search all you like, man. It's all gone.'

I nodded. 'You'd better be telling me the truth, Max. Don't let me down.'

'I won't. I won't let *myself* down, or my kids.'

I walked over and extended my hand to him. 'Shake on it.'

He looked at my hand, and then looked at me. In this interaction, I was the biggest threat to him. I was another Alpha Male invading his territory. I wanted us more on an even keel. Max was used to dealing with women, and I got a sense that he could be quite a charmer when he wanted to be and was not beyond playing the little-boy-lost card. But he was finding me much harder to deal with. He couldn't quite find an approach that he was comfortable with, and was veering from persona to persona, trying to find one that would get me onside. The man liked to be liked, but felt on very uneven ground with me.

He did not shake, but neither did I remove my hand.

'We can work together and try to get on, or we can pull against each other,' I said, 'but either way I'm in your life for the foreseeable future. It'd be easier if we could reach some kind of understanding.'

He laughed drily and took my hand, shaking vigorously. 'You're a tough bastard, Shane, but at least you're up front about it.'

I grinned. 'I bet you say that to all the guys.'

He laughed aloud at that. It would be one of the few moments of humour and friendship before the darkness fully descended.

Forty-five minutes later I was sitting in Josephine's office. She had asked me to come up and had welcomed me in. She was now sitting behind her desk reading the report on my one and only visit to the Kellys.

It was a lengthy paper because I was convinced that an investigation into the circumstances of the events would follow. I wanted to make sure that I had every point covered. After all, this was a visit that had involved a social worker, a community childcare worker, the gardaí, the psychiatric services and the ambulance corps. A woman had drawn a knife and had ended up cut, albeit shallowly, and had subsequently been temporarily committed (apparently she was due to be released back into society the following week). The social worker who was supposed to be co-ordinating things had had to be escorted home because he was obviously unfit to be on active duty. That left me the Senior Worker, and certainly the only competent worker, in situ. I was not taking any chances.

I sat and waited, looking around the office. It was decorated in a minimalist, almost spartan, manner. In Health Board offices, many features were the same. The carpet was a kind of dark beige carpet tile, the paint on the wall was the ubiquitous magnolia. The desk was standard also. On it sat a small clock that looked to be of Waterford Crystal, a laptop computer and a plastic cube that contained photos I assumed were of Josephine's family. On the wall was a simple print of a generic cityscape in a plain black wooden frame. Beside it was a large calendar advertising one of the local banks. It was almost as if she didn't believe that she'd be there for long, and had made no effort to make the space her own. Everyone else had tried to customise their desks and workspaces, so Josephine's lack of commitment stood out. I thought it was interesting, and decided to keep an eye on this lady. There was much more to her than met the eye.

She finally finished the document and looked up. Her eyes were a dark blue colour, giving her a deep, thoughtful appearance.

'Very thorough. You really did have quite a time of it, didn't you?'

'It was fun.'

She laughed in a brief snort.

'Fun is one thing I'm sure it wasn't. The Kellys are a . . . complicated bunch.'

'I gathered.'

'They have been on the books for a very long time, and there has been a series of workers involved to one degree or another, coming and going as the case moves through different stages and the focus changes from one family member to another. That's the way of it with long-term cases. You know that.'

I nodded. Continuity of care was always the aspiration, but often there was a rapid turnover of workers with families like the Kellys. When it became obvious that a family would be on the books for the long haul, the practice was usually to channel workers through a series of short projects. Staff would be circulated, moved on to other cases and other children, since these virtually permanent clients were seen as lost causes, simply being maintained – resolution of their problems was too much to hope for. Also, prolonged exposure could result in burnout, as had happened to Sinéad with the O'Gormans.

'This office is only concerned with the children in the family – other agencies deal with the adults. There are three minors in the Kelly home at present: Denise, who is seventeen, the baby, Christine, and Connie, who is fifteen. That leaves the parents and an older brother, Mike, who's in his late twenties and who has severe psychiatric disturbance. We, of course, have regular encounters with the other family members because of the nature of the work, but our focus is on the three minors.'

'I understand.'

'Denise has been the subject of several interventions, and we have managed to get her registered with a local youth project. Joe is in regular contact with the staff there, and Denise has a lot of support, so far as we can see. She has not exactly engaged with any of the workers she has been in contact with from *this* office, but we're told that she is contributing well to the classes in this placement, and seems happy there. She's attending regularly at least, which is more than she was doing at school.'

I continued to listen in silence. It seemed to me that the child and her associated problems had simply been passed on to someone else, but I kept that to myself and waited to hear where I fitted in to all this.

'Christine is still an infant. I can see from your report that she is physically thriving, but that the Kelly home is no place for her to grow up in. I could have guessed that without having read a word. Geraldine, Christine's mother, is an adult, and has a social worker attached from Psychiatric Services. I have spoken to him, and asked that he encourage Geraldine to move out as soon as possible, taking Christine out of harm's way when she does so.'

'Seems reasonable, although it stinks a bit of passing the buck.'

It was out before I realised I had said it aloud.

Josephine eyed me quietly, sucking on her lower lip. I wondered if I had made a major blunder. The silence dragged on for a long time, then she sighed and continued. Her facial expression and the tone of her voice did not alter one iota.

'You're right. I am passing the buck. We have an infinite number of cases and potential cases still in the referral stage which require investigation and support and a ridiculously limited number of staff. If there is another agency I can possibly bring in on a case to alleviate the burden, then I will. I'm a manager, and that's part of the job. You don't have to like all the decisions I make and you're welcome to question them when we're here. I welcome it, in fact. If you're asking me questions, then you're thinking. I just ask that you watch my back when we're out there and not question me at all if we're in the field. Are we clear?'

I felt suitably chastened, and knew that I had deserved to have rank pulled.

'We're clear.'

She nodded and continued without missing a beat.

'Connie is my real concern. She is attending the

local Tech, where her results are excellent. Her summer exams from the last academic year were all exemplary. She's expected to do very well in her Junior Certificate. The problem is that she seems to have shut down in every other way. She doesn't speak to her teachers unless it's to answer a question in class. There are a couple of girls she hangs about with during the breaks, but they're both kids with special educational needs, and it's as if she's only with them to keep herself busy and to feel wanted in some way. I doubt that they're meeting any of her social or emotional needs.'

'I don't know. Seems to me to be not unlike a lot of friendships you'll see among "normal" people.' I made inverted commas in the air with my fingers.

'Granted, but this is a bright kid. She's achieving A grades virtually across the board with absolutely no support whatsoever. Totally on her own, Shane. I mean, that's incredible, when you think about it. Like, how the fuck can she sit down in the insanity of that house and get stuck into algebraic friggin' equations every evening? The mind boggles!'

'Yeah, when you put it that way.'

'I want you to spend some time with her. Give the school a ring. Go out and meet her. Talk to her. Tell me what you think. I predict that some regular, safe contact would do her the world of good. Maybe you could organise to meet her at the school a couple of times a week to do homework.'

'Whoa, whoa!' I put my up hands. 'You know that

it might not even get to that. She might be terrified of me. You can't rush into this type of thing, Josephine, in all fairness.'

She laughed and stood up, brushing her skirt down over her thin legs.

'Sure, go on out and see what you can do. Nothing ventured, nothing gained.'

The meeting, it seemed, was over.

I stood outside Gillian O'Gorman's school, watching the students stream out in a steady flow of purple.

There she was.

She spotted me and stopped in her tracks, then slowly walked towards me.

I had rung ahead and told Sister Assumpta to let Gillian know I would be meeting her. I had owed the nun an apology. On investigation, I discovered that she had indeed been calling to ask for assistance with Gillian. Because there had been no worker directly appointed to the case, the calls had been logged but set aside until the O'Gormans had been allocated to someone's caseload. Assumpta had accepted my apology gracefully and made no further comment on it.

I had been wondering how Gillian would cope with the news that I was coming. I thought that she would either walk out of the school and pretend I wasn't there or would attempt to get out by another exit, maybe even by sneaking over the wall. I dealt with the latter option by asking Assumpta to have her walked to the main gate so that I could intercept her if she did decide to flee. It seemed that, on consideration, she had decided to at least confront me.

'What do you want?' she asked.

'I told you I'd be working with you. I'm here to start.'

'Sorry, I don't need anyone.'

'Sorry, I think you do. We're going to go and get a bite to eat. I've had a busy morning and I missed lunch.'

A look of panic spread across her face and she, impossibly, actually got even more pale.

'I am not fuckin' eatin'! You can't make me. I'll scream and scream and tell everyone you're tryin' to rape me, and then if you still make me eat I'll just puke it up again and you can't stop me from doin' that!'

'I tell you what. Let's start this off all over again. Walk with me.'

She set her face into a scowl, but followed as I began to walk towards the main street of the village.

It was a sunny but cold afternoon. I was wearing jeans, boots, a black woollen jumper and a long leather jacket. She was dressed only in her school uniform. I thought about offering her the jacket, but she would have looked ridiculous in it, like a child dressing in one of her parents' clothes. I made a mental note to get her a coat from the office petty cash the next time I saw her.

'I'm going to be coming out like this for a while.

I'll meet you after school, a few afternoons a week. We'll spend some time together, and I've organised for you to catch a later school bus back home. You won't be on your own with me; we'll be somewhere where there are lots of people. There's no need to be afraid of me. I won't hurt you. I don't hurt kids, like I told you last time.'

'I've heard that before. Don't mean nothin'.'

'It does with me.'

'Yeah, right.'

'Well, you'll just have to take my word for it until you can see I'm telling you the truth. Now, about the eating. I can see fairly clearly that you haven't eaten, or at least haven't held anything down since we talked last. For me, right now, that's the thing I'm most worried about. You have to start eating, Gillian.'

'No,' she whined. 'I won't!'

We had reached the main street and I steered her towards the small local café. I had already paid a brief visit, and had found what I was looking for on their limited menu.

'I'm going to take this slowly with you. Today we're going to have some soup. You are just going to have a small bowl. A kid's portion.'

'I'll puke it!'

'For today, that's allowed. I just want you to *eat* it.'

She looked at me with suspicion.

'You don't mind?'

'Well, obviously I'd prefer it if you didn't, but we need to take small steps starting out. We'll have a

97

meal together today and get to know each other a little better. You can do whatever you want after the meal. If that includes making yourself vomit the food back up, then that's your business.'

'Okay . . . I s'pose . . .'

'Good. We're here.'

The café was a small, one-roomed affair. It had a wooden floor, small tables with kitchen chairs and chequered plastic tablecloths. A small counter stood at the rear of the room with plates of scones, pies and fairy-cakes on top of it. A girl in her early twenties lounged at the cash register, her head buried in an issue of *Hello*.

Gillian and I sat near the door. An old lady was sipping tea at a table near the counter, but other than that the place was empty. When the waitress seemed not to notice our arrival, I cleared my throat loudly. This elicited a reaction: she looked up and saw us. Her spotty face registered a complete lack of interest and she sighed and hefted herself off her chair and made her way down to us.

'Yeah?'

'Could I have a bowl of vegetable soup please with a couple of slices of brown bread. I'll have a black coffee with that, and a glass of water.'

I looked at Gillian. I wondered if she'd order for herself and wanted to give her the opportunity to do so. She looked into space, however, and didn't move or make a sound. The waitress sighed again in impatience and irritation.

'Anythin' else?'

'Yes, please. We'll have another bowl of soup, just a half portion, please, and another glass of water.'

'Right.'

She walked quickly back to the counter and disappeared into the enclosed kitchen area. At least we wouldn't have to wait long – she would want to get back to her magazine as quickly as possible.

'So how have things been at school? Did you and what's her name . . . Maggie isn't it? Did you have any more clashes?'

'What?'

'Have you had any more fights with her?'

'No. She's left me alone.'

'Good.'

'Everyone has left me alone. They all think I'm mad, so they do. I don't care.'

'Don't you have any friends?'

'Yeah, I hang around with Trudy Tanner. But she's not in school all that much. She's deadly. We have a right laugh. She understands.'

'Understands what?'

'How things are.'

She said it so matter of factly that there was no room for further questions on the subject. It seemed that Gillian and this Trudy girl had worked out the meaning of life but were keeping it to themselves. I made a mental note to find out who the Tanners were.

'I met your mum.'

No response. Eyes directed out the window, watching the occasional passerby on the quiet village street. Evening was coming down fast and a slight mist was settling on the cobbled thoroughfare outside.

'I know you haven't been to see a doctor.'

Still no response.

'I've asked Andi to go with you tomorrow. She'll pick you up from school.'

Still no response.

'I told you that we had to do this, and I told your mum too. I don't lie. You're going to see the doctor, Gillian. Okay?'

She turned to face me, and I saw, for the first time, resignation.

'Okay.'

I sighed gently and smiled at her.

I didn't know what I had done to get through to her. While I was glad that she had acquiesced, it would have been good to know which act or combination of actions had been right, so that I could attempt to repeat them. The only thing I could think of was the fact that I had been consistent. I had said that she would see the doctor and had followed through on that. There was little enough constancy in her life, I supposed; when some filtered in, it was welcome. I had, however, worked with kids where this was certainly not the case, children who found consistency and normalcy so terrifying that they attempted to create chaos so that they could feel safe. I do not fall into the school of thinkers who believe that human behaviour is always predictable. I was well aware that Gillian responding this way did not in any sense mean that she would behave in the same way the next day – maybe it was better that I didn't know what had produced the response. Sometimes it's possible to be *too* analytical.

Our waitress approached.

'Good. Here's the food.'

Gillian's face dropped, but I ignored it.

The waitress dumped plates, bowls, cups, cutlery and bottles of water unceremoniously onto the table and stalked back to her post. I arranged things in front of us. The soup was a rustic, home-made vegetable soup. Its aroma wafted up at us from the deep bowls. I picked up my spoon and sampled the fare. It was hot and pleasant, if a bit bland, but I knew that enough protein, vitamins and nutrients would be in it to do her the world of good if I could get her to keep it down for any length time at all. A puréed soup would take very little time to digest, so a lot of it would go straight into her system.

Gillian was looking into the bowl with an expression approaching horror on her skeletal face. I looked at the soup spoon that sat on the table before her and reached over and took it. I gave her instead the teaspoon that had come with my coffee. Expecting her to use a soup spoon was simply ridiculous. She looked up at me and tears welled in her eyes and dribbled silently down her cheeks. I grinned at her reassuringly, knowing that this was a huge challenge for her. There was no pretence to hide behind, no bravado any more. I patted her gently on the hand.

'Slowly. One spoonful at a time. Little sips.'

She nodded, sniffed and picked up the teaspoon. She sat with it in her hand for a moment, looking at the steaming food. Then she dipped the spoon into it, the tip of the utensil just breaking the surface, and took it back out lightly coated with soup. Not exactly what could be called a spoonful. Her face had an expression of such utter distaste etched onto it that I felt truly sorry for her, but I did not relent.

'Go on, Gillian.'

She looked at me, still crying silently, and smeared some of the puree onto her lower lip. I saw her tongue dart out and lick off the offending material. We had begun.

I chatted about trivialities throughout the meal, every now and again coaxing her on. I ate, but hardly tasted what I was eating, my attention focused completely on her and her progress. I knew that she was never going to finish what was in the bowl, not today, but I was committed to sticking with it for as long as was feasible. I knew that eventually she would be able to stomach no more, and that I would know when that time had arrived. I felt admiration creep over me again for this child. She was trying so hard, struggling to overcome this terrible thing. Her will was amazing to witness.

When she had consumed around half of what was

in the bowl, she let the spoon fall on to the tabletop. We had been sitting in the café for close to an hour. She picked up her water glass and gulped a few mouthfuls. Her face had taken on a greenish tinge, and I knew that critical mass had been achieved.

'You want to go to the bathroom.'

She nodded vigorously.

'I'm letting you go today, like I said I would.'

More nods. She was beyond the power of speech, the urge to purge herself of the soup like a physical pain.

'The next time I come out with you, you keep the food down. I want you to promise me you'll try. We'll work on this together, and y'know, I think we might just be able to beat it.'

'Okay. I need to go now.'

'Go on then.'

In her urge to get to the toilet, she didn't even bother to close the bathroom door. Sounds of gagging and something splashing into the toilet water could be heard clearly. The waitress looked around with the same bored look and returned to her reading. The old woman seemed to be asleep and made no show of having heard a thing. I sipped my water and waited. After a few moments there was the sound of a tap running, then Gillian reappeared, looking sheepish and wiping her mouth on a piece of toilet paper.

'Feeling better?' I asked.

Her eyes seemed to be full of tears again, but I

wasn't sure whether that was from vomiting, or if she was actually crying.

'I couldn't help it. I wanted to keep it down, but I just had to . . . y'know . . .'

'Yeah. I know. You'll do better next time.'

'I'll try. I ain't promisin' nothin'.'

'All any of us can do is try, Gillian.'

'It's hard.'

'I know. You okay? We have to get you to that bus.'

She nodded.

I took money from my pocket to pay for the food, and then we walked slowly to the bus stop. Nothing was said during the short walk, and she climbed on to the bus without saying goodbye or even looking back at me. Words were not necessary. I knew what she was thinking, because I was thinking it as well.

There was a long road ahead of us, and neither of us knew if we were equal to the challenge.

5

Connie's school looked as if it had been built in the early 1970s – it had that 'bungalow bliss' design to it. As I made my way to the Principal's office, I was struck by the lack of religious adornment on the walls. I noted posters that encouraged students to 'just say no', to contact various agencies in the event of unplanned pregnancy or to eat more fruit and vegetables. A solitary crucifix, high above the school secretary's desk, seemed to be the only nod at Catholicism. Having been in Gillian's convent school with its stained glass and portraits of nuns and saints, it was quite a comparison. This school was obviously very different.

The Principal, a Mr Thomas, was in his late thirties. He had been in the job since the previous September, and was full of enthusiasm for his new post and dedication to the students. He was dressed in a cheap grey suit with the ugliest necktie I had ever seen.

'A present from my wife,' he explained when he noticed me looking at it. 'It's hand-painted.'

I nodded in commiseration.

His desk was a jumble of papers and books, some of them piled precariously. I could just about see him around one of these constructions as he took his seat.

'So you want to talk about Connie Kelly.'

'Please.'

'Well, she's a great kid. I've got her last set of results here somewhere.'

He poked through a bundle of loose papers and produced a black ring-binder. The act of pulling this to the surface caused one of the towers to collapse. He smiled sheepishly and arranged the detritus back into some kind of order.

Connie's grades were indeed excellent. She had achieved 'A's in everything except Irish language studies, and in that she had scored a B plus. The teacher's comments on her report cards were all complimentary but vague, seeming to be based on a glance at her grades rather than any real knowledge of her as a person: *Good student. Working hard. Always punctual.* I finished reading them and commented: 'She's doing great academically. Do you know her at all?'

'I taught her English when she was in First Year.'

'How did she come across in class?'

'I don't believe I ever heard her speak up over the year I had her, unless I asked her a direct question.'

'How did that strike you?'

'Many students are quiet, Mr Dunphy.'

'Shane, please.'

'Shane, every class has those students who are willing to speak up, who will draw attention to themselves – both for positive and negative reasons – and those students who prefer to sit quietly in their places and work. Connie belongs to the latter group. She is a very accomplished student, but a very shy young lady.'

'Does she mix well with the other members of her class?'

'Well, you'll have to talk to Ms Duff about that. She is Connie's Year Head, and will be able to tell you much more than me.'

'I'd appreciate that. One further question, if you don't mind. Have you had many dealings with Connie's family?'

'In the three years Connie has been here, there has never been any representation from her family at parent/teacher meetings. I am aware of the Kellys, obviously, but we have not taught her siblings at this school, and I have never met her mother or father.'

'Is that unusual?'

'My predecessor may well have met them when Connie came here initially, but that would have been before my time.'

'Thank you for your help, Mr Thomas.'

'I'll call Ms Duff.'

Ms Duff was a narrow-lipped, tightly wound woman in her forties. She sat with her hands clenched in her lap and looked nervous throughout our meeting. I was beginning to realise that any new information about Connie would not be gleaned from the teaching staff.

'Connie is a wonderful girl, Mr Dunphy. Hard-working, conscientious, supportive to her fellow students.'

'I've been told that her closest friends are students with special educational needs.'

'Yes. The two girls she is closest to both face certain challenges. Connie has been instrumental in assisting them in their work. It is most unusual to see such altruism in a young person.'

'So she spends time with these girls to help them, rather than spending time with her other friends.'

'Well . . . I'm not sure what you mean.'

'You just said that Connie was being altruistic by spending such a lot of time with the girls you mentioned. Altruism suggests sacrifice for no personal gain. I must assume then that Connie is giving up spending time with her other friends – friends of a similar academic ability – to help the students who need such assistance.'

'Well perhaps altruism was the wrong word.' Ms Duff wrung her hands, her discomfort apparent.

'Does Connie *have* any other friends, Ms Duff?'

'I don't know . . . I'm sure she must have . . .'

'Who does she sit beside in class?'

'Jessica Tobin usually . . .'

'Is she one of the kids we've been discussing?'

'Yes.'

'She associates with Jessica and this other girl . . .'

'Lizzie Kinsella.'

'Between classes, in the yard, that kind of thing?'

'Yes.'

'Does that seem odd to you? There is, of course, absolutely nothing wrong with Connie spending some time with Jessica and Lizzie. It's admirable and decent. But to spend all her time, to never want to be with anyone else ... that's unusual. At least, I think so.'

Ms Duff said nothing and appeared to be on the verge of hyperventilating.

'Could I see her now please, Ms Duff? You told her I was coming?'

'I'll get her from class.'

'Thank you, Ms Duff. You have been most help-ful,' I lied.

Connie was a small, portly, mousy-haired girl with thick glasses. The uniform of this school was grey, with a blue shirt and green tie. She looked at me unblinkingly and neither said hello nor offered me her hand. Connie did not seem bothered by my pre-sence. She didn't seem to be glad I was there, or happy, or sad or angry or excited. If I hadn't known better, I would have thought that *she* had special educational needs. She was like a *tabula rasa*.

'Do you know who I am, Connie?' I asked.

'You're a social worker.'

'No, I'm not. I'm a childcare worker. That's very different.'

'It's not. You're from the Health Board. You'd like to take me into care. You can call yourself anything. You're all the same.'

This was all spoken with a pleasant smile and a sweet tone. Just good pals talking about day-to-day stuff, shooting the breeze.

'Is that what you think?'

'It's what I know. I've had social workers coming and going all my life. I don't mind.'

'I'm not sure what to say to that, Connie. I mean, I haven't come out here to try and take you into care. It never even occurred to me—'

'You were out in the house a few days back, right?'

'Yes, I was.'

'Mammy took a knife to herself, right?'

'Yes, but—'

'You had her committed, didn't you?'

'I did, but—'

'I'm a child living in that house. Mammy has psychiatric problems. Daddy has psychiatric problems. My brother Mick, who lives in the house from time to time, has psychiatric problems too. Now, tell me that you haven't thought about trying to get me into care.'

I grinned. She had me.

'Fair enough. It probably did go through my mind.'

'I knew it. You're all the same.'

'Well, I'll tell you what. While we're on the subject, you tell me why I shouldn't put you in care.'

'Have you seen my results?'

'I have. They're all really good.'

'Except Irish.'

'B plus is really good in my book.'

'Doesn't matter. Are they the results of someone who's having problems? Do you look at them and think I'm badly adjusted?'

'I suppose not.'

'See. I'm getting on fine at school. Look at me. Am I undernourished?'

'No. Can't say that you are.'

'I'm overweight. It's hard to get exercise and study for the Junior Cert at the same time. I plan to lose some when the exams are over. Would you like to see my lunch-box? I have a perfectly well-balanced lunch – cheese sandwiches, orange juice and an apple. I am clean, my uniform is washed regularly and I have appropriate clothing for all weathers. See my shoes? Comfortable and sensible.'

She lifted her feet off the ground and showed me her shoes. They were sturdy black brogues. They didn't look new, but they were well cared for.

'Those are all the reasons why I don't need to be in care. I'm doing fine, thank you very much.'

'How are you getting on at school, and I don't mean your results. Do you have many friends?'

'I have two excellent friends.'

'Lizzie and Jessica.'

'Yes. Lizzie and Jessie.'

'Tell me about them. What kind of stuff do you do together?'

'We just do school stuff mostly.'

'School work?'

'Yes. The exams are coming up this year. We all want to do well.'

'That's great. So you help each other out and all?'

'Oh yeah.'

'How do they help you? You mentioned that you're not getting an A in Irish. Is it Jessica or Lizzie who helps you most with the Irish?'

The blank face returned. I had her in a corner, and I was fascinated to see how she would try to squirm out of it. What I was seeing here was a performance. All this confidence and self-assuredness was a front. Connie was so used to living under the threat of being removed from her home that she had created a public face. Here was a Connie for whom everything came easy, for whom nothing was a challenge. This Connie got good grades, had a well-balanced lunch, a washed and pressed uniform and sensible shoes. She even had the most difficult thing for a girl like Connie Kelly: friends.

'We help each other,' she said, the smile returning.

'Okay. If I were to ask to see Lizzie and Jessica's grades, would I see that these two girls are doing anywhere near as well as you are? Or would I see that they're in danger of failing all their exams? I'd bet the only reason they're not failing everything is because of the help that you're giving them.'

'They're my friends. I want to help them.'

'Fair enough. It's just that maybe you would benefit from having some relationships that involve a little fun. You're spending all your time doing your own work and these two kids' work as well. That's not healthy. I'm not saying not to be friends with them. I'd just like to see you having some times to relax, y'know?'

'I do relax.'

'When?'

'I don't know. At night.'

'At home?'

'Yeah, at home.'

'I've been at your home. I doubt that there's a lot of time to relax there.'

Silence. She blinked at me behind her thick glasses, not sure what to say next. I sat impassive, waiting for her next move. Connie Kasparov, chess champion.

'I don't need to see a social worker and I don't need to be put in care.'

I had her in check, and she knew it.

'Connie, will you stop worrying about being put in care! That isn't even on the cards at the moment. I've been asked to come out and spend some time with you. Be your friend.'

'You're joking me.'

'Nope.'

'I don't want you to be my friend! That's stupid! I mean, I don't know you, and I *have* friends. I don't need another friend – certainly not some stupid big social worker.' Her scorn was palpable. She folded her arms and crossed her pudgy legs, looking away from me in a furious sulk.

'I think I get the message, Connie,' I said, trying my best not to laugh at her righteous indignation. 'Let's try it another way. How about I meet you a couple of times a week to help you with your homework. You're so anxious to do well in the exams, and maybe I can help out. All the time you spend helping your friends is time you're not spending on your own school-work. We can meet here.'

She looked at me with deep suspicion. She knew damn well that there was an ulterior motive.

'You're not a teacher. What would you know?'

'I used to be a teacher. Not of secondary school kids, but I taught in college.'

'What did you teach? You don't look like a teacher.'

'What does a teacher look like?'

'Like Mr Thomas.'

'Mmm, you've got me there. But I was a teacher up until a week ago, I promise. What do you say? It can't hurt.'

'So it would be like a grind or something?'

'Exactly.'

'Are you any good at Irish?'

'Used to be. It'll come back to me.'

'I'll think about it.'

'I'll ring Ms Duff and organise our first meeting.'

'I said I'd think about it!'

'That B is killing you, Connie. You'll go for it.'

'You think you're so smart. You social workers are all the same!'

'Will you please stop calling me a social worker?'

I got lunch in a roadside pub and went back to the office. I planned to write up my Visitation Reports, read back over the Kelly file and prepare my first sessions with Connie for the following week. The weekend was looming and I was looking forward to putting the first week behind me and having a relaxed couple of days. My batteries were in serious need of recharging. I walked in the door of my office and, even though I should have expected it and been ready, the sight of Melanie lounging in my seat as she bellowed down the receiver of the office phone stopped me dead in my tracks and filled me with a black, bubbling anger.

The desk was scattered with open files and folders and her handbag sat on top of it all, spilling a deluge of tampons, lipstick and tissues.

'I know, I know,' she was saying, laughing raucously. 'Well we can meet tomorrow. There's a sale on in McClouds. They've got some lovely stuff in there. Why don't we meet there and we can go for a coffee afterwards and chat?'

I did it without even realising: I placed my hand on the cradle and cut her off.

She looked at me incredulously and stood up, dropping the receiver onto the desk with a clatter. We stood nose to nose, the aggression at last naked.

'What the fuck do you think you're doing?' she said incredulously. 'How dare you come in here and behave like you own the place? I was on a call! If you need to use the phone you wait your fucking turn.'

'I don't need to use the phone. I want to use my desk. Get out of my chair, get your shit off my desk and make your social arrangements somewhere else!'

She let out a deep guffaw and turned away, throwing her arms up.

'Your desk? This is *my* desk. It has been for the last two years and it will continue to be until I am good and ready to give it up. Which I probably won't, by the way. There are other offices in the building, Shane. Use one of those. And stop squeezing in over by the filing cabinet. You're getting in people's way!'

'My fucking files are in here!'

'*My* fucking files!'

'Melanie, you don't do this job any more! You are in another position, for fuck's sake!'

'This is my office, these are my friends and that is my filing cabinet with my files in it. If you open it up and have a good look, you'll see that I've been putting my new files in there too. The kids for the unit I'm setting up as part of my new post are staying in the refuge at the moment while a house is being made ready for them, and I shall be using this work space *at least* until the workmen finish on the house. You can like it or lump it, but that's the way it's going to be.'

'Melanie, I've been patient. I've moved aside and let you get on with it. But enough is enough. You gave up the job, and when you did that, you gave up all the perks of the job, like, for instance, the desk and the goddam office. I have a lot of work to do this afternoon, so move the fuck aside!'

'Shane, if you don't get out of my face, I am going to bring a charge of bullying and harassment against you,' she said quietly, coming in so close I could smell coffee and cigarettes on her breath. 'Just you push me one little bit further. I have carved out a nice little place for myself here. No one gets in my way, no one hassles me and no one ever, ever raises their voice to me or interferes with my business. You're new. I'll let you off this once if you just walk away . . .'

'For a job that's supposed to be about caring, social care attracts a hell of a lot of bullies, Melanie,' I hissed back, not taking my eyes off her. 'I've been facing them down since I was in college. Now, you go right ahead and bring your charge. I'll bring one right back at you. You're damned lucky I haven't brought one against you before now. God knows, I've had grounds!'

For the second time that day I seemed to find myself in a stalemate. We stood, eyeballing each other, neither giving an inch. The ice was broken suddenly by the sound of someone clearing their throat behind me.

I turned to see Francesca, another social worker, standing in the doorway looking bemused, if slightly uncomfortable.

'Umm . . . when you two are finished bonding, there's a call for Melanie. Mary Jeffries is on the line. She's just dropped into the refuge and there seems to be a problem.'

Melanie picked up the phone, placed it back on the cradle and pressed a flashing button above the dial. I realised that I was sweating profusely and that my shoulders were aching with tension. I flexed them and went into the kitchen, where I got some water from the cooler. I stood there, sipping, trying to calm myself. It was out in the open now, at least. Better to let these things out rather than leave them to fester.

Melanie appeared in the kitchen doorway.

'I need your help.'

'What?'

'The kids have become very distressed. Mary is up there, but the refuge staff can't cope. Francesca is the only other one here, and she's in court this afternoon. I wouldn't ask if there was anyone else. Would you come out and help me?'

'Do I hear a "please"?'

'Stop being a prick and come on.'

'I'd be delighted to.'

The refuge was a three-storey townhouse situated down an alley behind a car park on the east side of the town. Melanie pressed the buzzer and told the voice at the other end who we were. The door clicked open and we went inside.

The first thing I became aware of as we stood in the lobby was the sound of trampling footsteps upstairs, as if many people were running about frantically. The next thing was the sound of wailing and shouting. Behind this I could vaguely discern the sound of words spoken quietly and gently, each time being answered by more yelling and screaming.

'I see what they mean by "distress",' I said. 'It's six siblings we're dealing with, isn't it?'

'Yeah. It's been building all week. This will be their first weekend in the refuge. They were all in temporary foster placements, but those broke down. We thought that they'd do better together, but they just seem to be setting each other off.'

'It's another change. They've only just been taken into care. No matter how bad home was, that's going to be stressful. They were separated, so they act up and cause a stink. That breaks down and they all get moved here, which is stressful again. They're testing you, Melanie. How do they know you won't move them back home or start beating up on them or abusing them, just like whatever happened to them at home? You need to be watching out for the triggers. What are the things that set them off?'

'Everything seems to set them off at the moment! It's just been a tough week for everyone here.'

'I know how they feel. What ages have we got?'

'Three years up to fourteen.'

'Okay. Good broad range there. Let's go to it.'

We walked up a narrow set of stairs to a door with a key-pad outside it. Melanie punched in a code and we were inside the refuge proper. There was a hallway before us with doors leading off on each side, four in all. A flight of stairs led off to our left. Shouts and screams came from every direction. Out of the door at the very end of the hallway stormed a girl who looked to be around fourteen. She stopped dead in her tracks when she saw Melanie and me. This pause did not last for long, because in a second she turned on her heel and stomped back the way she had come, shouting: 'There's a fucking man in here! There's not supposed to be men allowed in here!'

'Why is it that I always seem to get that reaction?' I asked Melanie as we headed down the hall.

'Oh, it's your charisma. You're such a charmer.'

'You say the nicest things.'

The fourteen-year-old was standing in the centre of the room, screaming a torrent of abuse at a middle-aged woman with short dark hair, who was doing her best to reason with her in a gentle tone that was being drowned out by the adolescent's tirade. A little girl of about three was sitting on the floor among a scattered array of toys, sobbing and rocking.

'And look now. She's brought him in here! You told me that there'd be no men!'

I heaved a deep sigh, and clapped my hands hard. The sound echoed like a gunshot in the room and silenced the girl immediately. Even the child on the floor stopped rocking and looked at me open-mouthed.

'Could we stop shouting, please,' I said pleasantly. 'My name is Shane and I am a childcare worker. Whether I am a man or a woman is not important. Look at your sister, how upset she is. Let's all calm down and try to—'

The sound of thundering footsteps was heard as the other children realised that something was happening downstairs. Before I could get another word out, four children, three girls and a boy, exploded through the door in a barrage of noise and bluster.

'What's he doin' here?'

'Who the fuck is he? Babs, what's he doin' here?'

'I don't believe this shit!'

'Let's fuckin' kill 'em!'

Like a tidal wave, the volume erupted again and I saw that shock tactics and diversion would not work here. We had a long afternoon of work ahead of us if we were to settle these children.

'Any suggestions?' I asked Melanie as another woman came in, looking flushed and befuddled.

'Mary Jeffries,' she said, smiling meekly and offering me her hand. 'Thanks for coming.'

'Well, when my friend and colleague Melanie asked me so nicely, how could I refuse?'

The fourteen-year-old aimed a slap at my ear, and I raised my hand and deflected it. The boy, who looked to be about eight, tried to kick me. I side-stepped.

'I think we should try and separate them. They're totally unmanageable when they're like this and all together,' Melanie said, scooping up the three-year-old and handing her to me. 'Take Tina and Josh (she motioned at the eight-year-old boy, who was trying to pull a cupboard door off its hinges, probably to use as a weapon) and bring them upstairs. There's a worker up there, so you won't be on your own.'

I nodded and took Josh gently by the arm.

'C'mon. We're going to have a look upstairs.'

He turned and sank his teeth into my arm. My leather jacket took the brunt of it. I left him that way and half-steered, half-carried him out the door. Getting him upstairs was a struggle, because he went limp on the steps, lying there and refusing to move. Tina started to cry again and to struggle in my arms. I stopped trying to pull him up the stairwell and thought about what would be the most sensible approach to the problem. I left him there and ran up the stairs with Tina, finding the staff member and handing the child to her. Tina began to wail with gusto, but I figured that the staff member could handle it for a few minutes, and I went back to where I had left the boy. He was, of course, gone. I found him in a room near the entry door, where Mary was trying to comfort a little girl who looked to be five years old. The child was screeching inconsolably and flatly refusing to entertain any of Mary's overtures.

'C'mon, Lindsay. We'll sit down and have some tea and bickies and a wee chat, eh?'

'*No!*'

This negative exclamation was accompanied by a scream of such ferocity that I even saw Josh jump. He laughed to himself then, though, and launched himself right at Mary's leg, grasping her around the thigh and knocking her sideways. Lindsay turned and fled from the room, wailing profusely. Mary and Josh were a bundle of arms and legs on the floor. I covered the distance to them in a couple of steps and grabbed the boy around the waist, heaving him off the social worker and carrying him bodily from the room, his legs kicking, his arms lashing at my sides and a litany of invective pouring from him.

Getting him up the stairs without overbalancing was not an easy job. He was thrashing from side to side and when he realised that my falling was a possibility, he began to rock with even more ferocity, singing 'rock the boat' merrily to himself as he did so. I made it to the top and was about to relax when he went limp again, which meant I had to adjust my centre of gravity to keep my balance. When I did this, he grabbed the wall with both hands, and shoved backwards, attempting to push us both back down the stairs. I managed to just stop myself from falling by letting him go with one hand and catching hold of the bannister with the other. He giggled maniacally and began to use his head to thump me in the ribcage. I hefted him under my arm and moved up the corridor in a rush, dumping him on the couch in the room where the worker was cradling Tina. Thankfully Josh had worn himself out and stayed there, inert and panting. Tina seemed to have settled a bit, and was looking at me from huge blue eyes and sucking ferociously on a pacifier. Her pudgy face was tear-streaked and she was hicking from her recent crying session. My heart went out to her. She was far too young to have to experience misery like this.

The worker was a young woman who looked to be no more than twenty. She seemed to be shell-shocked by the week she had had.

'I only started here two weeks ago. I've never seen anything like this before!' she told me as I took Tina from her and we both eyed Josh warily. 'I didn't know that kids could be like this.'

'They've had a tough few weeks. They'll settle down. Don't be put off. You've probably seen the worst of it.'

Tina nestled into my chest and began to doze. I sensed something and realised that Josh was looking at me with intense hatred.

'Hurt her and I'll fucking rip your guts out.'

'I'm not going to hurt her, Josh. Did I hurt you?'

'You're too scared of me. They're all scared of me. I'm fucking mad, I am. I'll take 'em all on.'

'I'm not scared of you, Josh. You're frightened and angry and hurting. I know you just want to protect your sisters, but you don't have to here. No one will hurt any of you.'

'What's your name?'

'Shane.'

'Shane the pain. Shane with no brain.'

'Knock yourself out. I've heard them all. I could probably give you a few you couldn't think of.'

'I bet you love little kids. Want to ride us, do you?'

'No. I've heard that before too. You've probably had some nasty experiences with other guys. I'm not like that. But you have to learn that for yourself. It's okay to be mad at me right now. There isn't anyone else to be mad at.'

'Shut up!' he screamed suddenly and stood up.

'Just shut up! You're not my daddy! He'd fucking kill you if he saw you now with Tina. Let her go!'

He lunged for me again but I turned and he bounced off my shoulder and grabbed a fistful of my hair. Countless times I've wondered why I keep my hair long in this line of work. I should have tied it back when I knew there would be violence, but I didn't think of it. He pulled for all he was worth, and I felt my hair ripping at the roots. Then the worker was on him and he was fighting and swearing at her. She managed to dump him on the couch again and he sat there panting.

My mind was racing, looking for any way to defuse the situation. The refuge was not equipped for this. To properly restrain Josh would need at least two specially trained childcare workers. Melanie and I could do it, but she had her hands full downstairs. If I had a clear area and some mats, I could allow him to try and wrestle me and get it out of his system that way, once there was another worker present to see I was not hurting him or touching him inappropriately, but there was no such area. Some centres in which I had worked would simply have stuck Josh in a padded room until he had calmed down. I was desperately trying to think of something that the refuge might have that would help comfort this child. Suddenly, I had it.

'Do you have a PlayStation here?'
Josh looked up sharply.
'Why?'

'Because I feel like kicking your arse on it, that's why.'

There are certain things that are expected of the few males who go into childcare work. Most of us are expected to do the stereotypical things like taking kids to soccer and playing kick-about in the garden. We're expected to do things like carpentry. We're expected to love video games. As it so happens, I like none of the above, which has often proved a major disappointment to employers who have taken me on as the token male in the mistaken belief that I will fulfil these criteria.

In this instance, however, I thought that a bit of bravado would serve me well. Here was a way he could channel his aggression appropriately, and because I am absolutely appalling at these games, he would actually win convincingly without ever suspecting I was going easy on him. I am so spectacularly bad that no kid ever thinks I'm faking it.

Five minutes later we were seated in the TV and games room with a car-racing game playing. Josh seemed to have forgotten his anger and was explaining carefully the ins and outs of the game, giving a demonstration so I could see particular tricks and potential pitfalls to the track he had chosen for us. Tina was fast asleep on the worker's knee, and the worker herself seemed to be entering into a catatonic state now that an island of peace and sanity had been established in the refuge. Sounds of distress still filtered through to us, but they seemed to be lessening. Josh's demo lasted a full twelve minutes (he was an expert on the game, having done little else when not wreaking havoc over the past week), and by the time I was given a joy-pad, he was in reasonably good humour.

He won the first couple of games, but I learned fast and gave him a run for his money in the third. He looked quite impressed and even patted me gently on the back by way of congratulation. As we began the fourth game, Melanie came in, trailed by Babs, the fourteen-year-old.

'Well, I see you two are getting on fine.'

'Yeah . . .' Josh's tone was defensive, and I flashed Melanie a look to impress on her the delicate balance of our new-found relationship.

'Okay then. I'll leave you to it.'

Lindsay wailed past the door, with Mary still trailing after her, imploring her to have some tea and biscuits. Seconds later, Mary stuck her head in the door, looking close to tears herself.

'Mel, the lass doesn't want to talk to me. I've been following her around for more than an hour. Give her some time to settle herself. She can't keep it up much longer.'

Melanie nodded and Mary left, muttering something about needing a well-earned cup of tea herself.

Half an hour later I put down the joy-pad.

'Time for me to be making tracks.'

'One more game?'

'One more then. But after that I really have to go.'

'Will you come back? Play me again?'

'Aren't you afraid of me beating you?'

'No! Don't be an eejit!'

I laughed.

'Yeah, I'm sure I'll be able to call in again.'

I made my way slowly down the stairs to the kitchen. Melanie, Mary and the two workers were at the table, drinking tea. The next shift had arrived and were chatting with the kids. Melanie fired up a smoke and passed the box over to me.

'You did well with Josh,' she said.

'He's all right. Doesn't know whether he's coming or going. Looks like you did okay yourself.'

'I've been working with them for two weeks. I *should* be able to get around them at this stage.'

'I hate this job,' the younger worker moaned.

'Shut up, Biddy,' Melanie said.

'Can I talk to you for a moment,' I asked Melanie, 'in private?'

She nodded and led me out into the hallway.

'Listen, about back at the office . . .' I began.

'You shut up too. Here's where we stand: I'll be moving into one of the new buildings in two weeks. Until then, I will personally organise a desk for you in one of the other rooms. In a fortnight, I'll move all my *new* files out to the new place, and the work space is yours. Deal?'

I grinned.

'Deal.'

'Good. All it took was a fucking riot for us to learn to like each other.'

'Who said I like you?'

'Fuck off, Shane.'

'Charming. Last time I come out to save your arse.'

'Leave my arse out of it.'

And so my first week as a community childcare worker came to a close.

PART TWO

The Lost Fortnight

Where did you stay, my pretty little Miss?
Tell me, where did you sleep last night?
I've been in the Pen with those rough and rowdy men,
And now, I'm goin' back again.

'Hop High, My Loulou Girl',
Appalachian Mountain Song

6

Childcare is not like other work. Productivity cannot really be measured by normal means: there is, in fact, no tangible product at all. How do you chart the development of a personality or the gradual changing of an old mode of thinking? Is it possible to map out the altering of a way of life?

In the following months I slipped into the routines and practices of the work as if I had never been away from them. Childcare, particularly when it is community-based, has a rhythm. It is like a dance, or playing a piece of music. You become accustomed to the particular beat and fall in with it, because to work against it would be impractical and cause untold problems.

I also began to relish the small, almost imperceptible, signs of progress in the children I worked with. A smile; a less than violent response to a difficulty that would have previously provoked a bout of aggression; a passing comment that reflects previously unseen self-awareness: these were all reasons for celebration.

It was a satisfying time, and although I often worked alone, I enjoyed the camaraderie and professional companionship of the team during the times

I was back at the office or accompanying someone on a visit. I had struck up easy friendships with Andi, Betty and Marjorie almost immediately, but in the following weeks I also found a bond with Josephine. She had a steely intelligence and a genuine wish to improve the lot of the many children whose lives were in her hands. Her management style was very much collaborative, and despite the difference in rank, I never felt that she was looking down on me. I was given free rein on my cases, which suited me perfectly. She was always available to offer advice or support, regardless of the hour it was asked for, and I found that this offered me a safe and comfortable platform from which to work.

I had established a pattern for working with Connie. She needed a set routine, and I organised my diary around seeing her twice weekly. I decided that the school would not be a suitable place for these meetings. If I did my job correctly, Connie would be opening up to me, and when that happens it is impossible to know what may emerge. I didn't want her becoming upset at school, which she seemed to see as a safe haven, and where she might be seen by peers or teachers. I booked a room at the local health centre, and began to brush up on my Irish vocabulary and grammar. I did not really intend to spend much time on homework or study, but I needed to be able to at least follow what she was doing.

Connie remained extremely polite and good-natured, but closed off to me. The first four sessions, despite my best efforts, were stolidly academic. I found it very frustrating but realised that this young lady was experienced in evasion, and decided to just let our relationship develop at its own pace.

One evening, I arrived at the centre to find her already in the room, but without her books out as was her custom. She was sitting on the table at which we usually worked, her coat still on and her arms wrapped around her knees. I stood in the doorway, wondering what had prompted this change in behaviour.

'What's up?' I asked.

'Nothing. I don't feel like work today. You can go on.'

'Well,' I said, determined not to let an opportunity pass, 'why don't we do something else then? Do you want to go and get a cup of coffee, or go for a walk?'

'No thanks.'

'There must be something you'd like to do. Go and see a movie? Have a game of pool? Get a burger—'

'Could we go to McDonald's?'

This was uttered in a rush, like a small child who has suddenly been offered the chance to pick any sweet in the confectioner's shop.

'No problem. McDonald's it is.'

I'm not a huge fan of fast food, but you would be amazed by the amount of children I've worked with who have a deep fondness for McDonald's. I've come to believe that it's a symbolic attachment: the Golden

Arches seem to represent all the material things they should have received, but didn't.

Twenty minutes later we were there, with the familiar smells and design motifs and uniforms. I tried not to watch Connie too closely, but she was letting her guard slip and it was hard not to steal occasional glances at her. She was behaving as if it was Christmas morning and was giddy with excitement.

'What do you fancy?' I asked.

'I don't know. It all looks so good.'

'Absolutely. Well, people say that the burgers are pretty fine. Everyone talks about the burgers at McDonald's.'

'I know! But . . . the nuggets. When I was little my friends would always talk about the chicken nuggets . . .'

'Mmm. Well, why don't you have a burger *and* some nuggets?'

She looked at me with such unrestrained joy that I couldn't help grinning myself.

'Could I? Really?'

'Sure. No point in having one and then wondering what the other is like. I have a friend who can never decide on a dessert when we go out to eat, so one day she just asked for a little bit of all the deserts on the menu. Solved her problem right off.'

'They gave them to her?'

'She got a funny look from the waiter, but they gave them to her, yeah.'

'If I ever go out to a fancy restaurant, that's what I'll do,' she said with deep seriousness.

'So, a burger, chicken nuggets and some fries. Would you like a Coke?'

She didn't answer. Her gaze was fixed on a father and child at a table near us. The child was opening a brightly coloured box and taking out a small toy wrapped in clear plastic. Connie's mouth was hanging open, and without realising she was doing it, her hand reached over and tugged my sleeve.

'Shane,' she said.

'Yes, Connie.'

'Could I have a Happy Meal?'

I could have slapped my forehead at my own stupidity. Of course she wanted a Happy Meal. It was obvious from the start that Connie was playing out a deep-rooted childhood wish. Visits to McDonald's were either so rare as to be huge treats in the Kelly household, or had been totally non-existent. As a child growing up in a house where the television was constantly on, Connie had been barraged by regular McDonald's advertising. She had seen her friends bringing back Happy Meal boxes and toys, heard about birthday parties held at the local McDonald's – had lived in a world where this place held such glamour and excitement that it became to her a kind of wonderland. She now wanted to experience all the things she had craved as a five-year-old. Only a Happy Meal would suffice.

'Of course you can have a Happy Meal, Connie. You go on and sit down. I'll bring it down to you.'

I ordered a chicken nugget Happy Meal and an extra burger with cola and a cup of coffee and a burger for myself. Connie took the box and carefully opened it, removing the toy and placing it solemnly on the table before her. I watched her. It was, for a few moments, as if I wasn't there. She laid all the food out and studied it. She then sampled each item, taking small, dignified bites and a sip of her soft drink.

'Good?' I asked.

Beyond words, she nodded.

I ate my burger and drank my coffee and waited for her to emerge from her reveries. When the food was gone, she took the paper that had held the burger and placed it in the waste-bin, but she took the toy, still in its wrapper and put it back into the cardboard box of the Happy Meal and closed the lid. She was not throwing that away.

'Thanks, Shane, for bringing me here,' she said at last.

'No problem. Any time you want to, we can come. Just let me know.'

'You mean it?'

'I do. It's probably not good to eat here every week, because the food is fried and the drinks are full of sugar, but once every couple of weeks is fine, I suppose. If you want to come more often than that, we could just have juice or coffee. They do salads, but you probably aren't a big fan of them.'

She shrugged.

'How come you didn't want to work today? It's not like you.'

'I just wasn't in the mood for it.'

'Why? Did something happen at school?'

'No. School's fine.'

'At home then.'

There was no response, which was answer enough. She was sitting with her arms folded on the tabletop, her chin resting on them. She seemed suddenly lethargic, as if her excitement had worn her out.

'What happened at home, Connie? Is your mum upset again?'

She shook her head and buried her face in her arms, hiding her eyes.

'I guess you aren't ready to talk to me about that yet. And it's okay. When you're ready, I'll be around.'

She peeped over the top of her sleeve at me.

'There's nothing to talk about. You know what my family is like. Sometimes it just gets hard, that's all.'

'I can imagine. It must be very difficult.'

'Usually I can handle it. Last night it just got a bit much for me. Mam and Dad were shouting, and Mick started up then. He howls in the night sometimes, like a wolf. Long, long howls. Even though I know it's him, sometimes when he does it late at night it wakes me up and I get afraid. He just seems to be so . . . mad. Crazy, y'know?'

'I know. It must be scary.'

'And then I can't get back to sleep, and I lie there and I wonder if maybe I'll go mad living with them all. I've heard of people who go into nut-houses and they might be only a bit mad going in, but they end up totally crazy after a while in there. What if I end up like that? I'm okay now, but will I go mad eventually?'

'No, Connie. That won't happen. It doesn't work like that.'

'Sometimes, when it gets really bad, if they've been wound up a few days running, I sleep in one of our neighbours' houses. There's this old lady, Mrs Jones. She's always been nice to me. She used to give me biscuits when I was little, and I used to go the shop to get milk for her. She lets me sleep over sometimes, when I'm afraid to be at home. I like it at her house. It smells kind of funny, but it's so ... *quiet*. Do you know, she doesn't even have the telly on that much? She likes the radio, and she listens to this really old music on it. It makes me think of those black-and-white movies they show during the day sometimes – I've seen them when I'm sick and off school.'

'She sounds like a very nice person. You're lucky to have a friend that you can go to.'

She nodded and laid her head back down again, looking wistfully out of the window at the street.

'Oh, I'm not lucky,' she said. 'I've never been lucky. Not in my whole life.'

*

I worried about Connie, maybe more than the others. It wasn't that her situation was worse – far from it. It was that she seemed somehow less damaged than the rest of my clients. She was, however, teetering on the brink of the abyss. She had, through sheer strength of character, managed to remain functional and maintain a public face of calm normality. None of the rest of the kids I worked with had been able to do that. Gillian was obviously in deep trauma. Cordelia overplayed the maturity card, and seemed strange and remote. Connie, in stark contrast, was personable and pleasant, if a little shy. The display in McDonald's and the subsequent disclosure made me see what I had suspected all along. There was a damaged, frightened child inside her, screaming for help and attention.

I decided the following day that a visit should be made to Doonan. If the Kellys were in crisis again, maybe I could help. I recruited Sinéad to accompany me, as she had experience with the family, and we drove out that evening when we both had some space in our diaries.

The light was beginning to dim when we turned into that desolate estate. This time there were no children playing in the street. It seemed that everyone had taken refuge from the advancing shadows. There appeared to be little life in the Kelly house. No shouting, no lights on, the curtains drawn in the living room.

The silence was beginning to get eerie.

'What do you think?' Sinéad asked as we waited for a response to our knock.

'I'm reserving judgement,' I said.

No answer came, and I knocked more loudly. Muffled movements came from within, and a dishevelled young man opened the door. He wore a nondescript shirt and jeans, and looked like he had just risen from bed.

'Yeah?' he said, rubbing the back of his neck and sniffing loudly.

'Hello, Mick,' Sinéad said. 'We were just passing, so we thought we might call for a visit.'

Mick made a hawking sound in his throat, gurgled and spat something onto the doorstep. It landed with a dishearteningly heavy sound. 'Sure you'd better come in, so,' he said, turning and shuffling into the hallway, which was in total darkness.

The living room wasn't much better, although it was lit with the orange glow of the television and the incandescence of the fire. The vast bulk of Mrs Kelly was seated on the couch, exuding menace. She looked over at us as we entered, but said nothing, her gaze turning back to the television immediately. A grey-haired man was in the armchair adjacent to her. He was dressed in a tweed jacket over a string vest and dark-coloured trousers. A non-filtered cigarette smouldered in his hand. He nodded at us but also made no comment.

Sinéad perched on the couch beside Mrs Kelly. I leaned on the wall by the door. There was something wrong. It was far too quiet. I could feel the hairs on the back of my neck begin to stand on end. The atmosphere in the house was thick with tension. Sinéad sensed it too. I saw her shiver and shake her head to clear it.

'So how have things been, Mrs Kelly?' she asked, her voice full of levity and high good humour.

'Mmm,' Mrs Kelly said, her eyes still locked on the television.

'And you, Mr Kelly. I haven't seen you in a long time.'

'That's right,' the older man said.

I squinted through the gloom at the father, and realised that he wasn't watching the television at all, despite the fact that he was facing it. His line of vision was actually fixed on a point just to the left of it, on the far wall. I wondered how long he had been sitting there like that, staring at nothing.

Mick sat on the other side of Sinéad, and began to giggle. It was a horrible sound. There was no mirth in it, no happiness. It was a sick sound, as if all the foul energy in the house had found form and was spilling out of this young man. I wanted to turn tail and flee, get away from that sound of illness, but Sinéad kept it together and turned to Mick, looking perplexed but not at all bothered.

'God, Mick, that's a great laugh you're having. Do you want to share the joke?'

In the light thrown by the television, I could see Mick's face. His eyes were locked on to Sinéad, and there was no laughter in them. They were full of violence and rage. He shook his head at Sinéad's question and the giggling continued, rising and falling, then reaching an insane peak.

'Ye're all very chatty today,' Sinéad said over the cackling.

I knew that the bubble would burst, and it did right then.

'Jesus Christ, Michael, will you shut the fuck up!'

Mrs Kelly roared like a bull elephant and moved with frightening speed, reaching across Sinéad and grabbing her son by the throat with her massive hand. The manic laughter turned to gurgles, and the two fell back on top of the unfortunate Sinéad, who was caught between them.

I had no time for thought. I jumped across and got Sinéad around the waist. She was a tiny creature, and I pulled her out from under Mrs Kelly without much difficulty. Luckily all of the huge woman's attention was focused on throttling her son, so my actions went unnoticed. I was peripherally aware of Mr Kelly still perusing his patch on the wall with rapt fascination. Sinéad was gasping for breath and was trembling, but I dumped her unceremoniously onto the floor and tried to pry Mrs Kelly's fingers from around her son's neck. I might as well have been attempting to pull a brick from the centre of a wall. Her grip was ferocious. I had managed to loosen one finger when her dull gaze slowly turned and registered me. Her left hand, which had been lying unused in her lap, shot out and I was sent reeling across the room, landing in a heap against the armchair that her husband was sitting in. My weight and the force of my fall caused the chair to roll a couple of feet on its castors. Mr Kelly remained in exactly the same position, moving only his head so that he could see that spot of wall that so consumed him.

I pulled myself on to my haunches as quickly as I could manage and prepared to spring again when I realised that Mrs Kelly was no longer strangling Mick. The two were now seated side-by-side, looking at Sinéad and me in our various states of disarray on the floor. It was like being looked at by a couple of pit bulls, and I was convinced that we were in very serious trouble.

Then the laughter began again. Not just Mick this time, but Mrs Kelly as well. Hers had a deeper, more throaty timbre, but was no less terrifying for it. They looked at us, then at each other and as they did so the laughter became more and more hysterical. I reached over and took Sinéad's hand, and we slowly backed out of the room. I was expecting them to come at us any moment, and was ready to take whatever action was necessary to get out, but they never moved. The few seconds of almost pitch blackness in the hallway were like an eternity, then Sinéad was fumbling for the handle of the front door and we were out. Neither of us hesitated. We ran full-belt for the car.

Ten minutes later Doonan was only dim lights in

the rear-view mirror. My breathing had returned to normal and Sinéad had stopped shaking.

I looked at her.

She looked at me.

All we could do was laugh — and maybe we cried a little too. Sometimes it's hard to tell the two apart.

I tried to see Gillian as often as possible. I experimented with easy-to-eat foods, basically anything that did not involve chewing. So I brought her custards, mashed potatoes, creamed rice, puréed fruit.

One day I bought a book on weaning babies that had a variety of recipes. I went shopping and took over the office kitchen that afternoon, experimenting. When I had a good selection, I set up a taste-test for the staff. I wanted the food to be as inoffensive as possible, but I also wanted to start building her up to solids, so I tried to pack in some flavour, getting as much protein, fibre and as many vitamins into her as I could. I needed to know what she would be likely to eat and what she would turn up her nose at.

'Okay, I want people's opinions on these. Gillian is going to get thoroughly sick of veggie soup, and she isn't a big fan of chicken, so we're quite limited in what we can do. She seems to have a sweet tooth, and has been going for custard, especially chocolate flavour.'

'Do you have any of that here?' Melanie was in for a visit and was perusing the bowls I had arranged on the counter.

'No.'

'Damn.'

'I've labelled the bowls, so everyone please have a taste of each and tell me what's good, what's okay, and what's not so good. It's a crucial time for her now. She's holding food down and I don't want to lose her before we've begun.'

'Do you really expect me to eat anything that contains liver?' Sinéad was looking with undisguised horror at a brown concoction that I had labelled 'Liver, carrot and onion.'

'It's full of iron, Sinéad, and is actually not bad. I'm trying to get as many nutrients into her as I can.'

Sinéad spooned up some of the liver and let it dribble back into the bowl.

'You have *got* to be kidding.'

'This is surprisingly good,' Josephine said, looking at the inscription on the bowl she was trying. "Courgette and banana". Who'd have thought?'

'Yeah, I had some of that too. It's really nice,' Francesca agreed.

'This is to die for,' Melanie said, having a second taste of a bowl of 'Strawberry fool'. 'Got any more of this?'

'No. I've only made samples.'

'Could you make some more?'

'No!'

The exercise proved fruitful, and I went home that day armed with a database of good meals for Gillian.

Gillian herself was thriving. Her weight was increasing, and she had developed into a warm, friendly, open child who seemed anxious to talk. We met in different places: at the school; at the park; at her home. I left it up to her. While our conversations were hardly deep yet, I felt that a solid foundation had been laid for a genuinely therapeutic relationship.

I pulled up outside her house one Tuesday evening. It had been a grey, overcast day, and the threatened rain had just begun to fall. I sounded the horn and the door of the cottage opened, Gillian's small frame silhouetted in the light that emanated from inside. I turned up my collar and ran from the car. The dogs growled at my passage, but were all sheltering in the derelict car, and made no move towards me.

I got inside and grinned at the girl, immediately registering that something was not as it should be.

'Hey there, Gillian.'

She sniffed at me, and walked towards the living room. I stood where I was, the door still open and the rain coming in. I closed it and followed her.

'Gill, I've brought you something new to try.'

I had a tupperware bowl of the courgette and banana purée, as well as a pot of strawberry fool, which she had sampled the previous week and enjoyed.

'Lovely.' The voice was not Gillian's.

Libby sat in an ancient armchair in the room they used as a living area. In the few weeks I had been coming here, I had only met her that first time. I was struck again by her rough beauty, and was also immediately aware of the smell of whiskey.

'Hello, Libby. It's good to see you again.'

'The feeling is mutual, my lad. Getting on well with my little girl, are you?'

I didn't like where this was going, so I decided to steer the conversation as far away from my work with Gillian as possible. The girl was standing behind her mother's chair, as if she were on guard. I was reminded of the dogs outside, and how they had responded when Libby had come out to talk to Andi and me: silent, but coiled for action at the first signal. Gillian was looking at me, but her look was not friendly.

'How have you been, Libby? Are you working?'

'I've got a waitressing job at the hotel. Started last week. Don't know if I'll stick it though. Don't like the hours.'

'Yeah. That kind of work can be tough.'

'Like you've ever done it!' Libby and Gillian spoke the words in unison, as if they had been rehearsed. There was even a snort of derision at the end of the sentence that was uttered in stereo.

I blinked, unsure of what I had just witnessed. Libby laughed and reached to the floor for her glass and bottle. She poured a shot and raised an eyebrow at me in offer. I shook my head.

'Too strong for you, boy?' The last word was spoken with such dripping disdain that I suddenly knew how a black person must feel when addressed that way. I felt my anger rise, but pushed it back down.

'I'm working, Libby.'

'Is that what you call this? Jaysus, it's a grand thing to be paid to socialise, isn't it?'

'We're socialising, are we Libby?'

She didn't answer, but had a long pull of her drink. She took the whiskey like it was water, drinking it as if she were thirsty.

'Say what you have to say to my daughter, young fella, and leave us alone.'

I knew that I was wasting my time. Gillian was a statue behind her mother, looking at me with contempt and derision. I had got to know a young girl over the past few weeks, but this wasn't her. And this was no place for me. The ill-feeling directed at me was visceral and raw. I was still standing with the dishes in my hands, so I left them on a low table.

'There's some food there for you, Gillian. I hope you like it.'

There was no change in Gillian's visage. She remained stock-still, her hands resting on the back of the chair. I waited a second for some recognition that she had even heard me.

'What do you say, Gillian?' Libby said, pouring more of the spirit down her throat.

'Take your fucking muck and go,' Gillian droned.

I blinked in disbelief.

'What?'

In unison, this time: 'Take your fucking muck and go.'

I searched Gillian's eyes for any remnant of the

child I knew, of the relationship I had worked so hard to build. There was nothing there but hate and pain. Nodding, I picked up the containers again and turned to leave. Then I stopped and looked back at Libby. I spoke to her, not to Gillian. Gillian wasn't there.

'I'm going now. But I'll be back. And I'll keep coming back, Libby. For her.' I gesticulated with my head at Gillian, but kept my eyes on her mother. 'Not for the reasons you think. Dammit, I don't even really care what you think. You've achieved nothing today.'

'She's my daughter, you cocksucker!' Libby hissed.

'Cocksucker!' Gillian snarled.

'I know that, Libby,' I said, and walked out.

I was halfway to my car when I remembered the dogs. They were almost on me, running at me silently, fangs bared.

'Shit,' I muttered and took off as fast as I could. The closest animal sprang, but for the first time that evening luck was on my side, and the chain pulled it up just before it struck. I leaned against the bonnet of the car in the torrential rain, panting and waiting for my heart beat to regulate. The door of the house was still open with the yellow light cascading onto the sodden yard. Libby stood there, glass in hand, looking at me. I looked back. No words were spoken, but I knew that the war for her daughter's soul had begun. She turned and the door closed. I stayed there for a while longer with the water running into my eyes, feeling utterly helpless.

*

It was six o'clock on a Thursday evening. I was sitting in the reception area of the Health Board offices nearest to the village where the McCoys lived. Cordelia was pacing the floor, checking her watch, looking out the large windows every few seconds. Victor was sitting beside me, engrossed in a Game Boy. Ibar had a plastic box filled with earth and worms that he had captured.

We were there for an access visit with Max. The visit was due to begin at five. Max had not arrived, and the caretaker was anxious to lock up for the night. Cordelia, however, had other ideas. We would, she told me, wait for him. So we did.

'We're going to have to go, Cordelia,' I said at last. 'They need to lock up the building. We've waited for an hour and a quarter, sweetheart. I'm sorry.'

'Right,' she said sharply, grabbing her coat and storming out of the front door.

I sighed and rubbed my eyes with the heels of my hands. Cordelia had begun to go through the adolescence that she had been holding off because of all the responsibilities she believed she'd had. There had been much storming and stressing and quite a few screaming temper tantrums. She regularly informed me that she hated me. Mostly, I was delighted that she felt she could relax enough around me to behave in this way. On the other hand, after a long day it was very hard to be pleased with having to deal with teenage angst.

'Come on, you two,' I said to Victor and Ibar.

The two boys stood up, both still completely invested in their activities, and allowed me to steer them out towards the car. I called down the hallway to the caretaker that we were leaving, and went out to the car park. And there was Max McCoy, leaning on his daughter's shoulder and drunk out of his mind.

'Hey kids!' he slurred, an idiotic grin on his stubbled face.

I felt Victor tense beside me and squeezed his arm gently to let him know I was there.

'Worms!' Ibar declared, holding the box aloft for his father to see.

'Cool,' Max said.

Ibar nodded and returned to the study of his invertebrate pets.

'Max, you're an hour late,' I said as calmly as I could. 'And look at the state of you! We've got to go. I'm not going to facilitate access with you in this condition.'

'Aw, come on, Shaney,' Max said jovially, swaying so badly that Cordelia staggered under his weight.

I reached over and steadied him, moving him to the wall. Cordelia was visibly upset and Victor was still rigid with nerves.

'Stay there,' I said to Max and went over and opened the car.

The kids got in.

'I'll be with you in a few minutes. I just need to have a quick chat with your dad,' I told them.

'Worms,' Ibar said very matter-of-factly.

'Indeed,' I said, ruffling his hair and turning back to the now horizontal Max McCoy, who had slid down the wall and was half-lying, half-sitting on the ground.

I walked over and squatted down beside him.

'I'm taking the kids back to Dympna's,' I told him.

'Can't I spend some time with them?' he asked, trying to focus his eyes on me and not really succeeding.

'Not when you're like this, no. This isn't the first time, is it?'

'Whaddaya mean, Shano?'

'This isn't the first time you've fallen off the wagon since we put the kids with Dympna.'

'Yes it is! Sorta . . .' he disintegrated into a fit of giggles, which in turn disintegrated into a fit of coughing. 'Do ya got a smoke?' he asked when he had recovered.

I took out a couple and lit them with my Zippo.

'Max, we can't do this any more. The kids don't need to see you in this condition.'

'What condition?'

'Pissed as a fart, that's what!' I said, exasperated.

'Oh.'

'I'm going to cancel access for the moment. I want you to get clean and sober, and when you can prove to me that you can stay that way, we'll start the visits again. Maybe that'll give you some incentive.'

'Listen, Shane, that's great. Could you lend me a few bob? I'm fuckin' broke, man.'

I shook my head. I was wasting my time talking to him and I knew it. I just wanted the kids to see that I was treating him with respect, despite his intoxication. I took out my mobile phone and called a taxi for him.

We waited with Max for the taxi to come. I hoisted him up and brought him over to the car and let the kids chat to him. He was drunk but was at least in good humour. I didn't think it would hurt. It took the car twenty minutes to come, and in that time we had a little access visit in the car park.

Though none of them knew it, it was to be the last time they would be together.

7

The incident at McDonald's proved to be the only real step forward that I made with Connie Kelly in those early months. I continued to see her twice a week. During this period, my Irish improved greatly. I'm not sure that hers did, and I'm certain that our relationship did not develop at all.

I made no mention of my visit to Connie's home, and she made no mention of her fears or of her sleeping arrangement with her neighbour, Mrs Jones. There were no further requests for visits to fast-food chains. As one week, then another, passed by and we remained at a standstill, I began to feel that the subtle approach was getting me nowhere. I would tackle the issue head-on.

The next session with Connie began as normal. We worked on some Irish poetry and I read through an essay she had written. She was in a quiet, pensive mood that day, and I felt that that was good. She seemed to have something on her mind. Maybe she would be pleased to talk about it. As we were packing up to go, I said to her: 'Connie, can I ask you something?'

She looked at me with suspicion.

'What?'

'How do you do it?'

'Do what?'

'Keep it all inside the way you do.'

'How d'you mean?'

'I was out at your house a few weeks back, after we went to McDonald's and you told me things were getting tough. I saw Mick and I saw your parents. I don't know how you can keep going. I really don't.'

She continued to put her books into her bag.

'Did you tell them I talked to you?'

'No. Things got a bit hairy before I had a chance to say anything.'

'Good,' she said, and slinging her bag onto her back, she walked past me out the door.

It appeared that she had nothing to say on the matter.

I drove back to the office that evening, going over the case in my head and desperately trying to formulate a plan. Eventually, as I parked my car outside the offices, I thought that I had something worked out. Inside, I made a pot of strong coffee and headed for the basement.

I had been told that the Kellys had been on the books for decades. That meant that there had to be records going back that far. I had been coming at the case from the front end, trying to help Connie by drawing her out. It was going nowhere. She either didn't want to talk or wasn't able to. So that left one other line of investigation. *Secondary research.* I would go back to the information on the books, and see if it told me anything that might help.

The files of all old cases were kept in storage under the building. Bringing my coffee with me, I switched on the light and descended into the small room. It was lined with row after row of dusty, gunmetal-grey filing cabinets. The naked bulb shed a circle of light over a small table in the centre of the room, but the rest was all in gloom. Footsteps overhead and the slamming of a door told me that Rosalind, the building's administrator, and usually the last to leave, had gone home for the night. I scratched my head and surveyed the scene. The term 'needle in a haystack' sprang to mind, but I lit a cigarette, and began.

It was easier than it looked. Whoever had organised the filing system had done a good job. Cases were filed first by year, then alphabetically, so it was simple enough to trace the Kellys from the 1970s onwards. I moved up and down the aisles of cabinets, piling thick files onto a trolley and moving on. When I had worked my way up to the period where the inforamtion I already had upstairs began, there was a stack of paper on my trolley several feet high and covering a period of more than two decades. I sat down and started to read.

The earliest files related to Mick. I skimmed over them. He was not really my concern, but I wanted to look at the family from every available angle. A very brief glance at the paperwork on him told a story of neglect, peppered with strong suspicions of physical abuse. There were doctors' reports, letters from teachers, a handwritten note scrawled on what looked to be a serviette from a youth-club leader, all speaking of bruises, cuts, abrasions that should not have been there. As the notes continued, psychiatric problems came to the fore. Schizophrenia is often not obvious until the onset of adolescence, and by the time Mick was in his mid-teens, he had become a very disturbed young man. It seemed that that pattern had continued into adulthood, with a fondness for alcohol and narcotics thrown in for good measure.

Side by side with Mick's story was that of Geraldine, his red-haired sister, several years younger. In many ways the story was the same. I riffled through almost identical letters and reports from various professionals. Then something different caught my eye. It was a short letter written to the Social Work Department by a pre-school teacher. She had been working with Geraldine, and wished to express concern about an ongoing problem the child was having. I checked the date on the letter and did some quick mental arithmetic. Geraldine would have been two and a half at the time of writing. I paused to light another cigarette and continued. The note had been attached to a hospital report, which appeared to have been inconclusive in determining the cause of Geraldine's problem. I flicked back to the letter from the pre-school. The child had been bleeding from the anus.

I went though the rest of Geraldine's files more carefully. There were two other references to suspected sexual abuse relating to Geraldine, both incidents of overtly sexualised behaviour at school. I made notes of the dates and of the name of the investigating social worker in each instance, and moved on to Denise, the next eldest sister.

More of the same. Denise had been hospitalised on several occasions with fractures before she was five years old. When she was six, she had been picked up by the gardaí wandering the roads near the housing estate, naked and confused. When she was ten, she had actually disclosed to a teacher that she was having regular sexual intercourse with Mick. She had subsequently withdrawn the statement.

I checked my watch. It was approaching ten o'clock. My throat was raw with cigarette smoke. My nerves jangled from too much caffeine and my stomach grumbled for sustenance. I hefted the finished files back onto the trolley and looked at the remaining pile, all of which related to Connie. I was on the home straight. No point in stopping now.

Over the next hour, a clear pattern emerged. Problems seemed to escalate with each child, as the psychiatric disorders in both parents and the oldest son became progressively more pronounced. As unpleasant as the upbringings of the previous children had been, Connie's was by far the worst.

A report from the Public Health Nurse showed severe neglect in infancy. Connie had had to be hospitalised at fourteen months with severe nappy rash and malnutrition. This had resulted in her being placed in temporary foster care, but she had exhibited such distress that she was returned home. She was expelled from her pre-school for excessive violence against her peers, with one child requiring stitches after having been bitten by her. Junior school proved to be little better. Displays of sexualised behaviour were common occurrences. Connie was eventually moved to another school after, aged seven, she had taken a four-year old behind the boiler-house and 'touched him inappropriately'. She was hospitalised again aged eight, this time with multiple abrasions and three broken ribs. The medical examination also showed severe vaginal bruising and tearing. She was placed in residential care, but ran away repeatedly and was returned home within two months. At ten years of age, she disappeared for two weeks. A chance visit from a social worker showed her to be neither at school nor at home, and her parents were unable (or unwilling) to disclose her whereabouts. The gardaí were contacted, but they were unable to help. Then one day, she was back – but completely transformed. The new Connie was the one I had met and was struggling with. She was no longer violent, angry, flagrantly provocative. This Connie was straight-laced and quiet, a conscientious student, well-mannered and gentle. It was as if she had been replaced by another child.

I sat back and rubbed my eyes, massaging the back of my neck with my left hand. What had happened? Where had she gone? Why had she changed so dramatically? It made no sense. When asked where she had been, Connie simply smiled and said that she had needed a break and had gone off, sleeping rough and having an adventure. Nobody believed this, but there was no other available answer.

I looked at the page and a half of notes that I had made. I now had many more pieces of the jigsaw puzzle. I understood the situation a lot better. But I also had more questions. Connie remained an enigma. There was one thing I did know, however: sexual, physical and psychological abuse were going on in that house. Connie was fleeing more than frightening noises when she went into Mrs Jones's house to sleep. I just needed to gather some evidence before I could do anything about it.

'Why do you do this work, Shane?'

I couldn't see Gillian, when she spoke. We were in the park, lying on the grass looking at the sky. We were head to head, so she was completely outside my line of vision. It was February, and the first tentative rays of spring were filtering through in the early afternoon. The sky was blue in places, with small grey clouds scudding across it as if they were running away from something. We had met for lunch. Gillian was back on solid foods now and had almost regained her former prettiness, although her eyes still had that haunted look. I had not expected the question. We had been playing the age-old game of looking for cloud shapes – a game I often felt had the potential to be a non-threatening Rorschach Inkblot Test. The problem was that I always became so involved in it myself I forgot to pay much attention or take any notes.

'I like it.'

'What do you like about it?'

'I dunno. How many other jobs are there where they pay you to do this? And I like to help people, I suppose.'

'Well, you've helped me, anyway.'

'You helped yourself. I just pestered you into doing it.'

'Don't put yourself down – that's what you always tell me, isn't it? If I say you helped me, well then you did.'

I laughed.

'Using my own lines against me, now. I'll have to be careful.'

There was a lull as we turned our attention back to the sky.

'That one kind of looks like Elvis,' I said, pointing.

'Sort of . . . I wanted to die, you know. When you came, that first day, I was thinking about ways of doing it.'

'Yeah. I kind of guessed that.'

'That's why I stopped eating, at first. It was easier than jumping in front of a car, and it gave me time to get used to the idea of dying. After a while, it's kind of like you're half asleep. Everything seems slower. Gentler. It's kind of what I always imagine being drunk would feel like.'

'Other people have told me that too.'

'But it wasn't fast enough. It was taking months and months. So I started to think of other ways. I was going to climb the tower at school and jump off. Or throw myself in the river. I read somewhere that drowning is the nicest way to die.'

'I think that's relative. It's probably nicer than being eaten alive by a pack of wild gerbils, but then most things probably are.'

'I think that cloud looks like a gerbil.'

'Where?'

'There.'

'More like a hamster.'

'Maybe. But then you came along. You made me so mad. And you drove Mammy mad too. I thought she was going to blow a gasket or something, that first day. But you just kept coming back. Why did you do that, even when I was horrible to you?'

'It's all part of the service, honey. If I can't handle a few names and a bit of attitude, I'm not really cut out for this line of work, now am I?'

'I don't want to die any more. Not today anyway.'

'Today is what matters. We'll worry about tomorrow when it comes.'

'That sounds too easy. It's a whatchmacallit—'

'A cliché? Yeah, it is. And you're right. It's not easy. Nothing you have done or have yet to do is easy. But you'll manage. And if it gets tough, I'm here. I'm not going anywhere.'

'You're really not, are you?'

'Nope.'

'You know when those boys . . . did what they did to me?'

'Yes.'

'I thought I would die then. It hurt so bad I actually thought that I'd die. And they had this shrink talk to me, and he used a cliché too. He said: "what doesn't kill you makes you stronger".'

She laughed, and I was surprised that it wasn't a cynical sound, but light and bubbly with genuine humour.

'How stupid can you get!' she said, still laughing. 'You can bet your arse *he* was never gang-raped. What doesn't kill you *doesn't* make you stronger. It just fucks you up something rotten.'

'Ain't that the truth.'

We looked at the clouds in silence for a long time.

I was to meet Gillian two days later outside her school. She didn't show. I wrote it off as teenaged absent-mindedness, and drove out to meet her at the house. There were no signs of human life out there, and lengthy sounding of the horn drew only noisy fury from the dogs.

Several days passed and I was beginning to worry. Enquiries at the hotel where Libby worked informed me that she was also gone, and it seemed clear that the two had done one of their trademark disappearing acts. I discussed it with Andi and she agreed.

'It's a fucking miracle it hasn't happened before

now. I'm guessing that you pissed Libby off so much that she tried to go straight for a while just to show you. How have things been going with Gillian?'

'Really, really well. We had something of a break-through earlier this week.'

'There you go. She must have told Libby. Mammy has taken her to get her away from you. Gillian is her property, you see. If she opened up to you, even a little bit, that's a part you have and Libby doesn't. That's more than she can tolerate.'

'Jesus Christ.'

'My thoughts precisely.'

'So what do I do?'

'Well, you could ring around the refuges, see if they've showed up there. That's where they usually go. Libby has been barred from a lot of them because of her absurd behaviour, so it probably wouldn't be too hard to find her. But my advice is to sit tight. They always surface eventually.'

'So I do nothing.'

'Try it. I bet you'll be good at it.'

I resisted the urge to find them. It was not easy. I regularly pulled over the *Yellow Pages* and turned to the phone numbers for the Women's Refuges, the receiver in my hand and my index finger poised to dial the first number. But I held firm and trusted that Andi knew what she was talking about – though she assured me she rarely did.

To my relief the call came a week and a half later.

'Shane, is that you?'

'Gillian! Where the hell are you?'

She told me the name of the town they had gone to.

'What happened? Why'd you run off like that? I've been really worried about you!'

'Can you come and get me? Mammy's drunk all the time and goin' with men. She's had me begging on the street for money for the booze. I don't like it here. I want to come home.'

'Yeah. I'll be there by lunchtime. Stay where you are. Will your mum take off if she knows I'm coming?'

'I won't tell her.'

'You will, Gillian, but that's okay. I'm on my way.'

The drive took me two hours. I rang the refuge and told them who I was, getting them to ring my office to confirm I was authentic so I would be allowed in when I got there.

The refuge was about a half mile outside the main part of town, in a quiet, residential area. A frightened-looking woman let me in and ushered me into the front office.

'Thank God you've come.'

'What's happened?' I asked, worried now.

'They're . . . oh God, I don't even know how to say it. That woman . . .'

'Libby?'

'She's very difficult. I don't think we've ever had anyone like her. She tried to bring men back here three times, and got very aggressive when we wouldn't let her in with them. And these were not *nice* men, Mr Dunphy. They were . . . gentlemen of ill repute.'

'Oh dear.'

'She has been extremely uncooperative. We would have had her removed if it weren't for the child. But the *child*, Mr Dunphy! She has become very distraught. I wonder if we should call a doctor for her. Or a psychiatrist.'

'What's wrong with her?'

'I don't know! You're the social worker.'

'I'm not a social worker. I don't mean it like that. What's she doing?'

'Come with me.'

I was brought down a long corridor that ran the length of the building. The place had a clinical quality I didn't like, all white walls and disinfectant smells. Gillian and Libby were in a room at the very end of the passage, as if they had been tucked as far away from the general population as possible. Libby was flushed and reeked of alcohol. She was sitting in front of a portable television set and barely acknowledged me. But my gaze was drawn to Gillian. Even though she had only been gone for ten days, the impact of that time sat heavily on her. I immediately regretted my decision not to look for them. Gillian had lost a lot of the weight she had gained. She was filthy and dressed in what looked like articles from a charity shop: ill-matching, garishly coloured clothes and an ugly, outsized pair of platform shoes that she tottered about on ridiculously. I was embarrassed for her. She had just started to take pride in her appearance again.

What struck me most about Gillian, though, was her face. There were scratches down both her cheeks that I guessed were self-inflicted, and she had an expression of such fear and anguish that I had to fight the desire to go to her and just hold her, hug away all that anxiety and unhappiness. I felt terribly angry with Libby. *Fuck you*, I thought. *We were doing so well. But you just couldn't leave well enough alone. You couldn't just let her be.*

I didn't beat about the bush.

'Libby, I'm taking you and Gillian home.'

'What if I don't want to go?' she retorted.

'Gillian wants to.'

'Gillian wants what I tell her to want. Isn't that right, Gill?'

Gillian looked like a startled animal and jumped at the sound of her name. She was pacing the room as if it was a cage. As I watched, she wrapped a strand of hair around her fingers and wrenched it out in a clump.

'See? She doesn't want to go anywhere with you.'

'For the love of God, Libby, will you let me bring you back home? Who's looking after the dogs?'

'I left them enough food.'

Gillian had begun to whimper as she paced, still ripping at her hair. Several patches of scalp were noticeably bald, and some of these had open sores where she had continued to pick at herself even after all the hair was gone.

'Please Libby, I'm asking you nicely.'

'Will you fuck off and leave us alone!' she shouted, turning on me sharply.

This was just too much for Gillian. She let out a blood-curdling scream and flung herself at the wall as hard as she could, thumping off it with force. She rebounded onto the ground but did not stop. She gathered herself up and rushed at the wall that was adjacent, slamming into it with her head.

'Now see what you've done?' Libby said, reaching over and turning up the volume of the television so that she could hear over Gillian's screaming.

For a second I really did not know what to do. I was appalled at Libby's attitude and sickened at Gillian's display of self-hatred. Without even realising I was doing it, I reached over and spun Libby's chair around so that she was facing her daughter, who screamed again and threw herself to the ground this time, smashing her fists into the tiles as hard as she could.

'Look at her, Libby. Look at what you're doing to her.'

Libby spat at me, catching me full in the face.

'It's you that's doing her, you dirty bastard,' she hissed and swung the chair back around to the television.

I wiped the saliva off with my sleeve and turned to Gillian, who was sobbing bitterly now and preparing for another assault at the structure of the building. Just as she was about to launch herself at the wall again, I stepped in front of her and she thudded into me. I was surprised at how hard she hit me, and staggered back with the momentum. She was taken by surprise and stepped back, looking at me with shock and horror. She didn't stop for long though. Her face crumpled and she bared her nails at me like claws.

'Bastard!' she howled and attacked me like a wild dog.

Her nails raked my cheek and she tried to bite me on the face, but I had her by the wrists and spun her so that her back was to me and her arms crossed over her front. She tried to butt her head back at me, but I raised my shoulder and stopped her, and dropped to the floor so that it would be harder for her to struggle. That infuriated her even more, and she screamed and kicked and bucked and spat as hard as she could. Libby turned up the volume as high as it would go. The refuge worker, who had been standing outside the door all this time, came tentatively in.

'Are you all right?' she shouted over the noise of Gillian's protestations and Libby's daytime soap.

'I'm fine. Would you mind staying until she calms? I need someone to witness that I haven't hurt her.'

The woman nodded and stood there, looking very uncomfortable.

Gillian was pumped full of adrenaline, and it took her forty-five minutes to wear herself out. When I felt her sag, I spoke very gently to her.

'I'm going to loosen my grip now, Gillian. I need

you to promise that you won't go off on one again when I let you go. Can you promise me that?'

'Yes.' Her voice was barely audible.

I let go of her arms and she slid off me onto the floor in a heap. There were no tears – she had none left to cry. She just lay there, inert.

I suddenly realised that my left leg had gone completely numb, and I had to ask the woman to help me to stand up. I hobbled around the room for a few moments until the pins and needles subsided.

'Well, are you ready to take us home now?'

Libby was standing by her chair, the television switched off, with an irritated look on her face.

'Whether he's ready or not, Mrs O'Gorman, you are no longer welcome here,' the woman said tersely.

'Get your things, Libby,' I said. 'I think you've outstayed your welcome.'

'Oh, Shane – they're in the back garden.'

Dympna smiled her dazzling smile at me.

I found the three children huddled under a grove of trees in the large garden. It was a warm spring evening, and we were sitting together on a bench that was suspended from a wooden frame by thick chains, making a kind of group swing. The sun was slowly sinking below the horizon. Ibar crawled over onto my knee and remained there. He was black from rooting in the dirt for millipedes, one of which he had cradled in his cupped hands. All of us were quiet as we watched the red disk dip below the rooftops, bathing us in a golden mist.

'Sunsets always remind me of Mummy,' Victor whispered, to no one in particular.

When Cordelia didn't respond, I said: 'Why's that, Victor?'

'Don't know. Just, when I see one, it always makes me feel kind of sad for her.'

Cordelia sat up and rounded on her brother.

'Ice-cream makes you feel sad for her, Victor. So does Kylie Minogue, snakes-and-ladders, Domestos and Marmite. You're so weird!'

'Hey, leave him alone, Cordelia,' I said, as gently as I could while keeping the reproach in my voice. 'He's entitled to his feelings. Okay, seeing as you seem to feel so strongly about it, you tell us what reminds you of your mum.'

'No!'

A sulky silence followed, during which Ibar held up his latest pet for me to observe.

'Lotsa feet,' he said earnestly.

'It's a "millipede", Ibar,' I said, knowing damn well that he would not even attempt the word. '*Mill-i-pede*.'

'Lotsa feet,' he said slowly back at me, looking at me as if I were the biggest idiot he had yet to encounter in his short life.

'Everything reminds me of her too,' Cordelia said, her voice thick with suppressed emotion.

'That's what I always mean,' Victor said. 'All those things *do* remind me of her. I can't help it!'

'She was always around, you know? We did everything together, so everything reminds me of all the stuff we did.'

'That makes a lot of sense,' I said.

'She wasn't just, like, my mum. She was my friend too, you know?'

'Tell me.'

'I don't know if I want to. It'll . . . make me cry . . .'

Silent tears spilled from under her eyelids and ran down her cheeks.

'There's not a thing in the world wrong with crying, Cordelia. Let it come. I think it's been waiting a long time to.'

'I miss her . . .' she said, squeezing the words out, and then the grief came in a tidal wave and immersed her, and she was unable to speak.

I wrapped my arms around her and Victor, who had gone limp and very quiet, and we sat there on the swing that gently swayed in the cool evening breeze as the sun continued its descent and Ibar looked impassively at his siblings and played with his Lotsa feet.

After a while Dympna came out. She assessed the situation, nodded to herself and scooped Ibar up into her arms. He went without complaint, holding the insect up for her inspection ('Ooo, lovely,' she said. 'We'll put him with the others.'). She took Victor by the hand and he allowed himself to be led into the house. I looked down at Cordelia, who had burrowed herself into my chest. My shirt was soaked through with her tears, but I made no comment. She would let me know when she was ready to talk.

Presently she sniffed and pulled herself away from me. I produced a small packet of tissues from my pocket and handed them to her.

'You came prepared,' she said.

'Used to be a boy scout.'

'I doubt that.'

'You know me so well.'

'You just don't seem the type.'

She dried her eyes and blew her nose, then leaned back into me. The sun was gone now, and the first stars were twinkling in the darkening sky.

'Starlight, starbright . . .' she said.

'What about the rest of it?'

'I've wished so many wishes that have never come to anything – I just don't bother any more.'

'Maybe your luck's changing.'

'I'm in foster care. My dad is a drunk and my mother is dead. My brothers are totally insane. I've got no friends . . . in fact, you're probably the best friend I've got, and you're paid to hang out with me. Hard to see any positive change in that story, wouldn't you say?'

'It's kind of a grim picture all right, when you put it like that.'

'What other way is there to put it?'

'Well, you're in a foster placement which is happy to take the three of you. That's very rare, Cordelia, believe me. You are actually really lucky to be still

175

together. And this is a really beautiful place. Your dad *is* drinking again, but I think he's fighting it as hard as he can, and he's doing that because he loves you and wants you to get back together again. Alcoholism is a disease, Cordy. Just like cancer or any other serious illness. He needs to get better, and when he does, you'll be back with him. Your brothers are interesting guys. Victor is very intelligent. He just finds it difficult to communicate sometimes. I think that the problems you've all had have left him nervous and afraid. Ibar is five. That's it. He's dealing with things the way a five-year-old does. The world is still a big, exciting, new place for him. He probably doesn't really get much of what's going on. Once he has you and Victor as constants in his life, he's happy enough. He needs to know he's loved and safe, that's all. And yes, I *am* paid to see you, but tell me: what time is it?'

'I dunno. Around seven o'clock, I think.'

'I finish work at five.'

'So why are you here?'

'I thought I'd go and visit some friends.'

She hugged me tight for a second.

'Hmm. You sure can talk the talk.'

'It's not just talk. Tell me about your mum. Was she like you?'

'People said she was.'

'Do you have any photographs?'

'No. Daddy got rid of any we had. He was in a bad way after she died. They were really, really in love.'

'Do you remember anything about when she died?'

'Yeah.'

'Want to tell me?'

'Okay.' Tears in the voice again, but she needed to get this out. She had been holding it in for too long and it was eating her up. 'Victor and me had been out with Uncle George, that's my mum's brother. I don't know where Dad was. We came back to the flat and he knocked and knocked, but there was no answer. He tried the door then, and it was open. We went in and she was lying there on the floor. I thought she was playing a game, 'cause I laughed and went over to her and shook her to get up. But she didn't move. Ibar was in his crib and he started crying, and then Uncle George got scared and he said the f word and started to shout. The ambulance came, and the guards came, and we stayed with a woman who lived next door, an old lady. Mrs Coveny, I think her name was. She smelled of wee and she made us eat cabbage. After a while, Daddy came and got us. And we drove for a while, and stopped and we were in a new flat, and we would stay there for a while and then move, and then we got on a boat and came here. He told us, eventually, that Mummy had taken too many pills by accident, and they made her sick and she died.'

'And what do you think about that?'

'I don't know. I don't know whether it was an accident or whether she was sad and did it on purpose or what happened. All I know is that my mummy is gone. And I wish every day that she wasn't, but it doesn't change anything. She's still gone.'

Dympna re-emerged from the house, carrying two mugs of steaming hot chocolate, and the moment was gone. We took the drinks and chatted with the good-natured woman about nothing, and after a while we went into the light and warmth and played Mono-poly and laughed and the pain was momentarily forgotten.

'I'm enquiring about a case you would have investigated five years or so ago.'

'Can I ask in what capacity you are making the enquiry, sir?'

I told her my job title, gave her the number for the front desk and waited for her to ring me back.

'Very well, sir. I'll put you through to the Criminal Investigation Department.'

I was passed around from one person to the next for twenty minutes until a male voice came on the other end of the line.

'This is Detective Inspector Jim Mitchell. You're asking about Beatrice McCoy?'

'Yeah. I'm working with her kids.'

'And they're in Ireland now?'

'Yep.'

'Is that useless arse of a father with them?'

'He is indeed.'

'He's still wanted for questioning over here, you

know. Shot off like a whippet from a trap after his missus turned up deceased. We were, naturally, suspicious.'

'Were the . . . er . . . circumstances of her demise . . . suspicious?'

'Coroner wrote it off as a suicide. Can't recall the exact details, but if you ring back in an hour, I'll have found the report.'

An hour later Inspector Mitchell filled me in. 'Accidental death due to an overdose of psychotropic drugs. Which is a nice way of saying she topped herself. Coroners will often put down accidental death to avoid any extra grief for the family.'

'Anything else on the report?'

'Lots, mate, but nothing you'd understand unless you've got a degree in medicine.'

'Paraphrase it for me.'

'He mentions substantial bruising around the chest and abdomen where it wouldn't be obvious when she was fully clothed. Common in cases of domestic violence.'

'Had there been any reports of domestic violence before this?'

'The McCoys were . . . I don't know . . . they were like poor white trash. A lot of drink, a lot of dope. Max was doing a little bit of running with some local gangsters. Nothing heavy. Dropping off packages, picking stuff up. He wasn't bright enough or reliable enough for anything bigger than that.'

'Could that be connected with his running rather

than Beatrice's death? Maybe he owed them money or something.'

'Who knows? He never saw the body. Her brother identified her for us. Neither he nor the kids were at the funeral. They just ran. To be honest, the case is closed. I just don't like loose ends. Max McCoy is a loose fucking end. I always promised myself that if he showed up on my radar again, I'd blow him right out of the water. And what do you know? Here he is.'

'He's doing a pretty good job of blowing himself out of the water now, Inspector. He's drinking himself into an early grave.'

'I see.' Silence down the line, just that gentle hum you get on international calls. 'Well, you tell him I was asking after him. And good luck with those kids. I hope it works out for them.'

'Me too.'

8

The note on my desk said: 'Shane, Gráinne Hartigan wants to see you as soon as you get in.' I read it three times, and it always said the same thing, so I got in my car again and went to see her.

Gráinne Hartigan was the childcare manager, meaning that she was the overall co-ordinator of the entire Community Care operation in my area. I had never met her before, and knew only that she was a psychologist by qualification and had a reputation for being forward thinking. She was, it was said, as focused on the real needs of the children as her position allowed her to be. This suggested that she was a decent person, struggling against an overloaded system to make a difference in the lives of the people with whom she worked. And she was probably failing wretchedly. I just hoped that she hadn't become cynical yet. It happened – I saw it all around me, in fact, among those who had been doing this kind of work without a break for ten years or more. It can eat you up if you let it. You begin seeing abuse and neglect everywhere and lose the capacity to function in the real world. You become the job. It's not a good way to go.

Gráinne was a tall, strong-looking woman with

steel-grey hair, cut very short and very close to her skull. In another person it would have looked severe. On her it looked just right. She projected confidence and intelligence. Coffee was already sitting on her desk, alongside a plate of miniature croissants.

'Have you had breakfast, Mr Dunphy?'

'No, ma'am – but this doesn't look like breakfast to me.'

She laughed and poured coffee into one of the hand-crafted pottery mugs that were on the wooden tray with the coffee and sugar and bread.

'How do you take it?'

'Black. Straight up.'

She motioned at the mug and I took it. The coffee was very good. I took a croissant and swallowed it. It was good too. But small.

'You're wondering, I'm sure, what I asked to see you about.'

'I think I know. You've read my report.'

She looked at me blankly.

'You seem to have me at a disadvantage, Mr Dunphy.'

'The Kelly visit . . . on my first day . . .'

She shook her head.

'I know of no such visit. I have seen no report.'

'Well then, ma'am, you have *me* at a disadvantage.'

'Shall we dispense with the formalities? May I call you Shane?'

'You may.'

'Thank you. I am Gráinne.'

We shook. She had a firm grip. I wasn't surprised.

'I wish to speak to you about Gillian O'Gorman.'

'Oh.' I was surprised. 'What do you want to know?'

'Tell me what you think of her. How is the case going?'

I told her what had happened between Gillian and me so far, leaving nothing out. She listened without a word, her hands steepled before her.

'And how has she been since you brought her back from the refuge?'

'Depends on the day. Yesterday she was glad to see me. We went for a walk, talked about school. She laughed and joked and was fun to be around. Two days before that she barely spoke to me when we met for lunch. She ate most of a ham sandwich and listened while I talked about this and that. Didn't even say goodbye when I left her off back at school.'

'What do you think this girl needs, Shane?'

'What she needs and what it would be possible to do for her are two very different things, Gráinne.'

'Did you ever watch Jimmy Saville when you were little, or was that before your time?'

'What?'

'Do you remember he used to have a television programme on a Saturday evening? *Jim'll Fix It*, I believe it was called.'

I laughed and nodded.

'I remember. I was only three or four at the time. I thought that was his name: "Jimell Fixit". I actually used to call him Jimell!'

'Well then, you know that children, and indeed some adults, would write in to him and ask him to organise for them to do things that they would normally never be able to do. Parachute jumps, be a clown in the circus, meet a pop star, that kind of thing.'

'Yeah.'

'Well, pretend I'm Jimell. What if I could fix it for you to get Gillian whatever it was she needed. What would you wish for her?'

'She needs to be away from her mother. That would be a really good start. I think that everything else would follow from that. She needs to be in care. A secure unit, if at all possible.'

'Very good. Now, suppose I told you that I could organise that – what then?'

'We would need to get her to go for it. *Making* her go would probably be more damaging than leaving her with Libby.'

'Definitely. So how would one go about doing that?'

I thought for a moment.

'I suppose it would need to be done therapeutically. She needs to see that her relationship with her mother is damaging and, that to get on with her life, she needs to effect a separation. The only way of achieving that would be through therapy.'

Gráinne was nodding, watching me working it out, listening to me thinking aloud.

'My thoughts precisely.'

'She hates shrinks, though.'

'Yes.'

'I could probably get her to see one, but the chances of a useful relationship developing are slim to none.'

'But she already has a relationship with you.'

'I'm not a therapist, Gráinne.'

She poured me more coffee and sat back, steepling her fingers again.

'Are you familiar with Freud, Shane?'

'Yes.'

'Have you studied the methods by which Freud developed the idea of the Oedipus complex?'

Gráinne was referring to one of the most famous theories in psychoanalysis. Sigmund Freud was an Austrian psychiatrist who did his most important work at the end of the nineteenth and the beginning of the twentieth centuries. He had proposed that children – let's use boys as an example, because he did – between the ages of three and six, experienced a powerful attachment to the parent or guardian of the opposite sex – in this case the mother. They then became jealous of the father, particularly of his relationship with the mother, which the little boy perceived as being far more powerful than his own. This eventually resolved itself, and enabled the child to form healthy relationships later on in life. Freud had constructed the theory through working with the son of a friend of his. He had never actually done any face-to-face work with the little boy, but had instead directed the father and received regular updates on how the work was going. Therapy by remote control, if you like.

'You're going to direct me?'

'Not me. I have a colleague who has done a lot of this kind of thing, particularly with staff and children in residential care. I think that you should meet her and discuss Gillian.'

'Okay. But I'm not committing to anything. This is . . . well it's very deep work you're proposing.'

'I know. I think she needs intense regression therapy. But I do think that you're the one who should do it. It sounds like she sees you as her saviour.'

'She thinks that at ten o'clock, but by lunchtime I'm just some arsehole who won't leave her alone.'

'She's conflicted, Shane. But that doesn't take away from the deep bond you've been able to build up with her. Let's use that to really help her.'

'I'll meet your colleague. I do, however, know my limitations. If I think I'll just fuck her up worse, we'll have to think again.'

'Fair enough.'

I stood to go.

'Why are you doing this, Gráinne? I thought Gillian was a lost cause, as far as the department was concerned.'

She smiled wistfully and looked out her window at the traffic humming past on the street outside.

'Once upon a time there was a young psychologist

who was sent a little girl. Her first case, in fact. This little girl was very damaged, very troubled. The psychologist did her best to help the girl. Used every trick she had learned at college. But she couldn't help her. There are some things they don't – *can't* – teach you at college, things you can learn only through experience. This is what she was lacking, though she didn't know it at the time. And often, in the years that followed, the psychologist would lie awake at night and think about that child and wonder what became of her. And every now and then, a file would come over her desk that reminded her of that particular girl, and when that happened, she would try to do something about it. We cannot save them all, Shane. But we can do our damnedest.'

I parked my car outside the cottage and checked the address that I had written in my notebook. I got out and went to the front door.

The house was like something out of Enid Blyton. Honeysuckle grew round the door and gnomes peered out from behind shrubs in the garden. A ginger cat stretched lazily in the afternoon sun. It felt wrong bringing anything unpleasant here. I knocked anyway.

An elderly lady answered. She looked to be in her late sixties or early seventies, but her face and her ease of motion spoke of a keen intelligence and a sprightly physical fitness that belied her advanced years. She looked at me expectantly.

'Can I help you?'

'Are you Selina Canning?'

'Yes.'

I told her my name.

'I'm a childcare worker with the Health Board. I'd like to talk to you about the Kellys. I believe you worked with them.'

She grimaced and sighed deeply.

'Yes. I did work with that family. But I have nothing to add to whatever exists on record. I haven't seen them in years, and I have not worked for the Health Board for a long time. I can't help you.'

She turned to go, but I put my foot in the door.

'Please, Ms Canning. I know that there's something really bad going on. The files hint at a lot of stuff, but that's all they do. What happened to Connie when she disappeared? Do you know?'

Selina Canning paused then, and opened the door just enough for me to enter.

'You'd better come in. That is a long story. And not a pleasant one.'

She sat me down in a living room that was as quaint and prettily designed as her garden. Prints from the Beatrix Potter books were on the walls. An upright piano with a white lace cloth over the top stood by the window. The room smelt of fresh flowers. A few minutes later she came in with tea things.

'Would you like a little whiskey in your tea, Shane? I'll be having some. I usually do, about now.'

It was just after two in the afternoon.

'Well, when you put it like that, why the hell not?'

When the tea was poured, she sat back and looked for a while at nothing, cradling the cup between her hands as if to warm herself, although it was not cold in the cottage. I sipped the tea. She had put a very fine whiskey into a small jug for us to dip into, and I bet that Libby O'Gorman would have given her eye teeth to have sampled some of it.

'I worked with the Kelly family for ten years,' she said at last. 'I am not ashamed to tell you that I never enjoyed my contact with them, and I never bonded with any member of that family. I found them all extremely difficult to deal with, and I believe that they always saw me as their enemy. I knew almost as soon as I began visiting the house that there were levels of violence and abuse at work that I would never be able to counteract. But what did I really expect? Psychiatric illness often manifests itself in that way, doesn't it? People hurt themselves and those around them. I tried to ensure that the parents saw their doctors regularly, and I set up various services for Michael – Mick they called him. But I saw no real change or improvement in any of them.'

'The children?' I prompted her.

'Yes. Geraldine was the first to exhibit signs of abuse. Her behaviour, you see. Back then, sexual abuse wasn't as prevalent or talked about. I thought that she was seeing things on the television, on those videos some people watch – they had such things in the house. I thought she was just copying what she saw. I talked to them about being careful, about not viewing them when she was in the room, but it was always a waste of time. Going through the motions. Then, a couple of years later, Denise told her teacher that she was involved in a sexual relationship with her brother. She wasn't asking for help, mind. It was more of a boast. The teacher in question was a young girl who was to be married. The children were going to sing at the church ceremony, and were all talking about how exciting it was and how she'd be living with her young man after the wedding. It came out then. As soon as I was called to talk to Denise, she said that she was only joking. What could I do? Her parents were virtually incoherent when I spoke to them about it. Mick became aggressive . . . and Shane, this was a different time legally. We didn't have the powers then that we have now. It wasn't as easy to take a child into care. Before the Child Care Act, the burden was on the child-protection workers to find proof of foul play. The parents' needs always came first. And there was no proof, just a ten-year-old girl's *fantastic* claims. In those days, an *adult* within the family needed to ask for help before social services could get involved in a case at all.'

I knew that it wasn't as simple as that, but I let it go. I wasn't there to point fingers of blame. I wanted to hear what she thought had been going on. I needed her to join the dots for me. I had my own suspicions, but she had been with this family for a decade.

'With Connie, everything was worse. The physical

abuse was worse. And she responded terribly. Denise and Geraldine were stoic. They never really caused much fuss. But Connie, she was a firebrand. A fierce child from when she was a baby. They say that infants learn early that their cries will not be answered, and become silent children. She never did. I remember her screaming constantly in the first couple of years of her life. The family hated her. And I will admit, she was hard to love. There were problems right the way up through school. Aggression, peer abuse. A tormented child, wouldn't you say?'

'She's quite different now, Selina. She changed, it seems, after this lost fortnight.'

She nodded and poured more whiskey into her tea. I was driving, and was only whetting my lips to keep her company.

'The lost fortnight. Yes indeed.'

'A missing child would have caused quite a stir. A lot of questions *must* have been asked.'

'Oh, we asked a lot of questions, Shane. You've got to understand, there simply weren't any answers. Connie Kelly, to all intents and purposes, disappeared from the face of the earth. It's not as if we didn't try and find her. The gardaí were involved, her vanishing was covered by the media . . . we put in a huge effort. But we didn't find her. Not until she turned up.'

'How did that happen?'

'She just came home. Or so we were told.'

'Was she dirty? Bruised? Emaciated?'

'No. She could easily have been staying at an hotel.'

'It just doesn't make sense.'

'Well, it does, in a way.'

'Explain.'

'She said that she had run away and had lived in the fields and woods nearby. A big adventure. They had been reading excerpts from *Tom Sawyer* at school, apparently. It had caught her imagination. This was total nonsense. There was no evidence to support the claim at all.'

'So what do you think happened?'

'She was sent away.'

'By whom?'

'Her parents and Mick.'

'To what end?'

'Within that past year, she had been getting more and more out of control. There had been severe problems at school, public outbursts around the town. Then she was beaten to within an inch of her life and ended up in hospital. I think that this was done to keep her in line, probably by Mick, but it could just as easily have been her father or mother. She was drawing a lot of attention to the family. The medical reports caused her to be put in care – the physical stuff plus the genital scarring was enough to have her removed from the home. But care couldn't hold her. There were no secure or high-support units then, and she just kept breaking out and going home. The decision was made to let her stay at home, and then, she disappeared. Does that seem a peculiar coincidence to you?'

'Maybe.'

'Do you recall the incident of Denise being found naked half a mile from the house?'

'Yes. I read the report.'

'How does a six-year-old end up naked half a mile from her home? No one saw her walking *from* the house. She was found trying to make her way *back to it*.'

'Oh Jesus . . .'

The puzzle started to lock into place, and I felt the colour draining from my face as it did.

'I believe that these children were being rented out. I think that Connie was sent somewhere very nasty, to show her just how tough it could get if she didn't play the game by the rules. And it must have frightened the living daylights out of her, because she never caused a single minute of trouble ever again.'

'You're suggesting that they're being used as child prostitutes.'

'Yes, I am.'

'Did any of them ever tell you this specifically?'

'No, they did not.'

'You have no proof.'

'None at all. But I *know*.'

I felt the bile rising in my throat and forced it down. The picture that had just been painted for me was too terrible to entertain. Yet it fitted. It all made an awful, warped kind of sense.

'Did you ever tell anyone about this? Your superiors?'

She nodded.

'And . . .'

'They asked me the same questions you just did about proof, and advised me never to commit my suspicions to paper.'

'Aw God.'

'I fear that He is no help to us at all, Shane. He has turned His back on those children. They have been left with no one.'

'That may be so, but we can't give up on them. I can't give up on them.'

'Ah yes. And what makes you think that you will be any more successful in making them listen than I was?'

'I can be pretty annoying.'

'Well, good luck to you. You have brought back quite a few memories I have spent years trying to forget, and have sentenced me to at least a week's worth of sleepless nights. If that is a small taste of your talent for irritation, well then you may just emerge victorious.'

She topped up both of our cups with whiskey and raised hers in a toast.

'May you give them hell.'

'I'll drink to that.'

And I did.

Max McCoy was hung over. It was obvious to me that he was, even though he insisted that he had a dose of the flu. His eyes were bloodshot, his breath stank of liquor and he held his head every time I spoke as if each syllable caused razor blades to grind together inside his skull.

'You're shitting me, Max. You're in the clutches of one bastard of a hangover and we both know it. Now, get some vitamin C and some Alka-Seltzer or some tomato juice and a raw egg or whatever the fuck it is you use as a cure and when you feel human we'll talk.'

He nodded and instantly regretted it, massaging his temples and moaning quietly. He stood and delicately left the room. I lit a cigarette and waited for him, talking to him through the open door.

'I didn't think that professional drinkers got hangovers. I thought that was a problem only we amateurs had to deal with.'

Mutters were my only response, so I followed him into the kitchen. With Cordelia gone, the house was not in a pleasant state: the sink was piled full of dirty dishes, the bin overflowed with rubbish, and foul dishcloths lay here and there in damp bundles. The whole place reeked of desperation.

'Didn't catch that.'

He was trying to drink a pint of water and seemed to be finding the experience less than pleasant.

'It all depends what you drink, how much and for how long.'

'Oh.'

'I always do badly on gin.'

'And you had some last night?'

'I've been drinking nothing else for three days.'

'If it makes you sick, why do you drink it?'

'Ever had a hangover?'

'On occasion.'

'Does something specific bring it on, or just having one too many?'

'Well, some things cause it worse than others, but I'd say that once I know I'm over my limit, I also know that I'll be a bit the worse for wear in the morning.'

'But it doesn't stop you from drinking again, and having one too many?'

'No.'

'It's the same for me.'

'Mmm.' I shrugged.

He drank some more water and belched loudly, holding his chest in discomfort. Acid indigestion, I imagined.

'We have something of a problem, Max.'

'What's this "we" shit?'

'I'm the one who has to tell your children why they're still in foster care.'

'Tough for you.'

'Yes, it is.'

He downed the rest of the water in a series of deep, nauseating gulps and slammed the pint glass down on the greasy, stained draining board. He looked at me with venom.

'Do you want to know why I hit the gin, Shane?'

'I do.'

'Not much gets me really comatose any more. It takes a lot. I needed to get very drunk very fast. So I got a bucketful of juniper juice and I got blotto. And I did it because this is fucking killing me. I can't stand to have them away from me, Shane. They're only down the road but they might as well be in fucking Brazil, because I'm not allowed to see them. My own kids! So I drink. And drinking means I can't see them. Catch 22, isn't that what they call it?'

'I understand, but you have to understand my position as well. While you're in this state, my hands are tied.'

'Smug bastard.'

What he said made me think. The problem was, I didn't really know how to solve the problem. By drinking, he was delaying his reunion with his children, but my decision not to allow access was causing him to drink even more heavily. I just didn't know what to do.

I sat in my living room that evening, Tom Waits playing gently on the stereo, singing about being wounded and wasted myself. I wrote a list of the pros and cons of the whole McCoy situation. To be honest, I was beginning to feel that I was trapped, whichever way I went. While it seemed that Max had been violent towards his wife, there was no evidence to suggest that he had ever been violent with his children. Neglectful, certainly. Psychologically abusive, definitely. But not physically violent. Was there an emotional bond between them? A very close one, but

I was not sure how much of that was insecure attachment. He had been the only constant adult figure in their lives since the death of their mother, and that would have contributed powerfully to the links between them. However, the children also had a genuine affection for Dympna, who was not likely to need to be undressed for bed or to have her vomit mopped up.

I was not foolish enough to underestimate the bonds of blood or the indelible imprinting between parent and child, though. I had worked with children in the past who had been unspeakably tortured by parents and who had gone back to them at the first available opportunity after having been taken into care – Connie Kelly was a clear case in point. I sat back and listened to Tom, who didn't sound in much better shape than I was: sometimes music says it like nothing else. It seemed that my clear task here was to get the family back together. The best way to do that was to give Max as much support as I possibly could to get off the alcohol, and to try and help the children develop a more healthy relationship with him. Cordelia saw him as a child and heavily idealised her dead mother. Victor seemed afraid all the time, worried about what Max was going to do next. Ibar had become totally self-sufficient, having learned in his five years that everything was transitory and nobody stayed around for long.

I needed to help these kids build up a set of

positive, real memories of their family. I pondered this. Where to begin? It seemed to me that the memories the children had were all a mix of fact and fiction, a mythology they had created between them to protect themselves from the grim reality. What were the touchstones I used when thinking of my own childhood? I suddenly recalled the conversation I had had with Gráinne Hartigan about Gillian. Her mention of a television programme had brought back a flood of memories. I saw myself as a three-year-old, kneeling in front of an old black-and-white television in the kitchen of my family's home on a grey Saturday evening as my mother busied herself with the evening meal. I smiled again as I thought of it. I would use the artefacts that all families have: songs, stories, places; I would encourage them to tell me all the little anecdotes that they shared. I would begin to build with the children a true image of their history, one that would encompass *all* their feelings about their father, mother and indeed themselves, both positive and negative. It was quite a task, but was absolutely necessary if they were ever to have a real relationship with their parents. And, anyway, if my meeting with Max that morning was anything to go by, I had plenty of time.

'Shane, I don't know who you've been talking to or where you're getting your information, but you are way off beam on this one.'

Josephine sipped her drink and gazed at me with no small amount of anger. The rest of the bar was empty, the after-work crowd not in yet.

'I spoke to the social worker who was on the case at the time. She's retired now.'

'And you took it on yourself to look this woman up and annoy the fuck out of her, did you? On whose authority? Did you do this during work hours?'

'Yes.'

'That's nice. That's really nice. The next time you want to play Philip fucking Marlowe, you check in with me first. I can't believe this!'

'It all fits. Have you looked at the file?'

'No, I have not! And I don't need to know that this is all the rambling of an old woman who sounds like she was at the sharp end of the job for far too long and has taken to romancing in her twilight years. You have fallen, Shane, for an urban myth. Paedophile rings and kiddie brothels! I'm not saying they don't exist, because they do, God save us, but what you are dealing with here is a fucked-up family. Is Mick abusing Connie? Probably, but you'll never get either of them to admit it.'

'Connie needs out, Jo. You know that.'

'They took her out and she kept running back. You just told me as much.'

'That means we give up on her?'

'Who's giving up on her? I told you to get out there and work with her. With *her*, mind, one-on-one. I don't remember telling you to go off on some half-arsed crusade. I really question your judgement on this one, Shane. Seriously.'

'I want to call a Case Review.'

'Why?'

'To see if we can't come up with some viable options for this child.'

'On what grounds? She's doing great! The only reason I sent you out there was to help her develop some social skills, for heaven's sake! Look at her grades, look at her appearance. What exactly are we going to bring to this conference, other than wild suppositions by a childcare worker and a woman who isn't even employed by the board any more! Why the hell didn't she bring this to anyone's attention at the time?'

'She did. Apparently, she got the same reaction I'm getting now.'

That caused Josephine to stop.

'Oh, well . . . I'll think about it. You understand how it sounds, don't you? I mean, Jesus, Shane. We'll come off like fantasists!'

'Josephine, I would rather look like an idiot in front of a room full of pen-pushers than leave this little girl in that situation one day longer than I have to. Do you understand where I'm coming from?'

'You'll be doing yourself no favours and you're not going to make any friends. This case has been knocking around for a long time, and a lot of the people sitting on the review board will have worked on it. You'll be telling them all that they were negligent in their duties. You'll be a pariah.'

'Seems a fair trade.'

'You're an awful arsehole. You know that, don't you?'

'Yeah. It's been pointed out to me before.'

9

Gráinne's colleague was a diminutive Jungian psycho-therapist named Maria McKinley. When I met her in a café in town, she was drinking espressos (she had five in the hour I was with her) and talking so fast that she gave me a headache. I am not self-conscious about my intellectual ability – I'm no Stephen Hawking, but I'm able to hold my own. This woman made me feel like a monosyllabic Neanderthal. I barely understood a single word she said.

Eventually, in total exasperation, I decided to bite the bullet and ask her to tell me, in plain English, what it was she was asking of me.

'Maria, unfortunate though it may be, I do not possess a PhD in psychology. Neither am I a Jungian scholar – I am aware of Jung, but know almost nothing about him. If I'm to do the work that you and Gráinne are proposing, you need to understand that, because I am having real difficulty understanding *you*.'

Maria blinked and raised her hand at the waitress for another espresso.

'Oh. I'm really sorry 'cause Gráinne told me you were a talented therapeutic worker and I just assumed that you were into Jung y'know almost everyone who works in this area is so I just made that assumption and I hope I haven't put you off or anything you see I'm really excited about working with you on this case it's a fascinating study!'

That was actually the shortest sentence she had spoken to me.

'Sorry to disappoint you. Let's start from the top. How does regression work, and why should I believe that it's not just a load of bullshit?'

That knocked the wind out of her sails completely.

'You . . . you think it's bullshit?' she asked incredulously.

'It does sound rather like it, yes. I don't see how playing at being a baby can help Gillian. I'm all for her experiencing things that she's missed, but as the person she is now. I'm really dubious about teenagers being encouraged to suck pacifiers and soil themselves. If a teenager is already sucking a pacifier as a comfort object, fair enough. But to suggest and encourage such a thing just strikes me as creating new problems.'

'Oh dear. I see we have much work to do . . .'

'Looks like it.'

When I went out to see Gillian two days later, I was armed with a working understanding of Jungian therapy and a slightly less dubious attitude towards it. I was still not one hundred per cent convinced, but I was prepared to try – besides, I was really worried about Gillian, and would give just about anything a go.

Since coming back from her excursion to the refuge, Gillian had continued to self-injure, and her mood swings had become even more extreme. I was beginning to believe that she was a manic-depressive. One day she would be on top of the world, bright and cheery, overflowing with things to say and visibly delighted to be meeting me. The next day she would be apathetic and lethargic, sometimes even openly hostile. I didn't need her approval, and had worked with children before who didn't like me, but I felt that these drastic ups and downs were neither normal nor healthy. Her body was a patchwork of bruising and she continued to pull out handfuls of hair when she became agitated. Something needed to be done, and I was at a loss to come up with any useful alternatives.

So I talked to Gillian about the possibility of doing some regression. Thankfully, she was in one of her good moods, and sat patiently with me by the stream that ran noisily along the south end of the park, listening to my suggestions. I did not tell her of our long-term plan to take her into care. She wasn't ready for that yet. I framed the proposal, simply, as a way of helping Gillian to deal with her current problems: her self-harming, the anorexia she continued to struggle with and the impact of her rape. The plan was to try and regress Gillian right back. We would create a womb using a round survival tent, which would be filled with warm pillows, blankets, duvets, whatever we could lay our hands on. We would set up gentle blue lighting and play soft, chordant, instrumental music (Maria had recommended whale music, but I thought this was just a bit too New-Agey, and would put Gillian off). During the sessions, which were to last forty-five minutes, I would bring Gillian through a series of guided relaxation exercises, many of which would involve visualisation and the use of her imagination. As the sessions progressed, we would bring her through infancy into later stages of development, using the same kind of techniques. I finished running through the plan with her, and awaited her response. She said nothing at first, sitting with her knees pulled up to her chin, tossing small pebbles into the stream.

'So, what do you think?'

'God . . . I don't know. It seems kind of weird. I mean, to bring me back to when I wasn't even born. Isn't it just kinda like playing?'

'It's exactly like playing. But there's nothing wrong with that. Playing is a fairly serious business, really. It helps us to learn about all sorts of things.'

'Have you talked to Mammy?'

'No. I thought we could ask her together. I'd like to do the therapy out at your place, if that's okay. This shrink I was talking to reckons it will work better if it's done there, because it's where you grew up and where you live.'

'Right.' She nodded.

'So? What do you think?'

'Do you think I should do it?'

'Do you want to know what I think?'

'I just asked you, didn't I?'

'I think that you're really, really unhappy at the moment, that you're in a lot of pain, deep down inside. In here.'

I placed my hand on my chest, over my heart.

'I believe that a lot of the pain goes back to when those boys hurt you, but I reckon there's more to it than that. I think there's stuff you don't even know about, and maybe this will help us to find what that is and start to deal with it.'

Tears welled up in her eyes, and she let them run down her cheeks, making no effort to wipe them away.

'I don't like seeing you hurting, Gillian. I'd like to at least try to take some of that pain away from you. Shit, this might not work. I'm not making any promises. But we can try.'

'Okay,' she croaked, sniffing loudly. 'Let's go and talk to Mammy.'

Libby was, amazingly, in favour of the idea. She listened to my explanation of the process in silence, nodding occasionally. When I was finished, she showed me a room at the back of the house that was full, from floor to ceiling, with junk of every conceivable kind.

'You can use this, Shaney boy. It's my box room.'

'Thanks. What are we going to do with all this . . . er . . . stuff . . . ?'

'I'm sure that the Health Board can stretch to hiring a skip.'

'I'll see what I can do.'

Gráinne laughed cynically when I told her of Libby's kind offer of the room.

'I suppose it's a win-win situation,' she said. 'You get a space to do the therapy, she gets a room cleaned out. She's a very manipulative lady is our Libby.'

'But oh so subtle.'

It was decided that I would begin the therapeutic work the following week, and would see Gillian every day from Monday through to Friday. Both Maria and I wanted to see if the methods we had settled upon would yield any fruit. The room had been cleared out, and I brought a vacuum cleaner and some detergents with me on Monday before Gillian arrived home from school to ensure that the area was as clean and pleasant as possible when we began. I set up the tent, lined it with the fabrics, put the coloured light bulb into the fitting, plugged in the portable stereo, lit some scented candles, and we were ready.

Gillian was very nervous and slightly embarrassed when she finally arrived. She was late, and I knew that she had purposely prolonged her walk from the road. She came into the room and giggled nervously.

'You want me to go in there?'

'That's what we discussed.'

'I don't know. I feel stupid.'

I thought we had a non-starter. She really looked terribly uncomfortable with the entire affair.

'Tell you what. I'm going to go out and chat to your mum for a bit. Why don't you hang out in here. It's *your room*. Your mum and me have made this special space for you, to do this work in. Spend some time here, maybe try the tent out – see what you think. I'll give you a few minutes, and check in with you. Take your time. There's no pressure at all.'

I went out to the living room, where Libby was watching *Murder She Wrote*.

'Did you ever wonder, Libby, how all these murders seem to happen when Jessica Fletcher is around?'

'It seems odd, all right.'

'Maybe she's actually a serial killer. She offs all these people, frames the guest star of the week and then writes her books about it.'

'When the show comes to an end they'll probably reveal that that was really happening all along. I wouldn't be surprised.'

I made my way back to the therapy room. Gillian was nowhere to be seen, but the flap of the tent was half zipped up, and I could hear gentle rustling from within. I walked quietly over to the stereo and switched it on at a relatively quiet volume. Then I sat down on a beanbag by the door, which I left open so that Libby could keep an eye on things.

'For today, Gillian, all I want you to do is breathe. You are in a warm, safe place. Nothing can hurt you. You have the sustenance you need. You are loved and wanted. You just have to *be*. Now, I want you to breathe in deeply, feeling the air fill your lungs . . .'

And the regression began.

When the first session was over, I told Gillian quietly that she could come out when she felt ready, and went back out to the living area, where I sat in front of the television with Libby. *Highway to Heaven* was playing.

'Michael Landon is so *nice*,' she said.

'He's nice. That's for sure.'

'I think he'd bug the hell out of me.'

'I think *you'd* bug the hell out of *him*.'

Gillian came out of the therapy room fifteen minutes later, wrapped in one of the blankets, and lay down on the couch. She looked flushed and tired. I wondered if she had been crying, but she turned her face into the back of the couch so I couldn't see.

I waited with them for another twenty minutes. Gillian didn't stir. Maria had warned me about this. Children who live in emotional turmoil often find the process of being still and nurtured disconcerting. I went over to her before I left and knelt down at her head.

'I'm going to go now, Gillian. I know you're probably feeling kind of strange, and that's fine. It's normal. I'll be here tomorrow afternoon, and we'll do some more. Do you feel you'd like that?'

A slight shrug of the shoulders showed me she was at least semi-conscious, so I took it as an affirmative and had Libby walk me past the dogs.

'So how d'you think it went then?' she asked as we stood at her door.

'We'll see.'

Libby nodded and said no more. I was extremely suspicious of her role in all this, and was waiting for her to try to sabotage it. It was very out of character for her to co-operate with anything I did.

I worked with Gillian every evening that week, as planned. Her response was less extreme each time we met, and by Friday she was chatting with us as she lay on the couch after the therapy was over. The following week, we met four times, and the week after that three. We would leave the frequency of visits at three sessions for a month, and then review our progress.

At the end of the second week I met Maria McKinley and Gráinne Hartigan for a working dinner. I was tired and heart-sore from the two weeks of work with Gillian, trying all the time to walk on eggshells around Libby – and my other cases had not stopped existing either. I felt as if I was being pulled twelve different ways at once, and was having trouble keeping any perspective.

'So how do you feel it's going, Shane, I am like so curious I could actually burst I mean have the methods been working is the child showing any signs of improvement do we need to reassess our plans or what have there been any ill-effects you've noticed how has her mother responded?'

'Maria – stop!'

She closed her mouth in mid-flow, blinking at me in embarrassment.

'Sorry.'

'It's Friday evening. I've had a long couple of weeks. Give me a second to get my head together.' I ordered a beer and took a long drink. 'Now, to answer your questions in the order I think you asked them, although where the question marks were, I'm not sure. I think that the therapy is going really well. In the two weeks we've been running the regression, there have been no mood swings or self-injuring at all. That's the longest period of calm I've experienced since I began seeing her. Despite initial discomfort with the process, Gillian has engaged fully, and has shown no severe ill-effects other than moderate disorientation immediately post-therapy, which is normal. Libby seems to be still working with us, and is not trying to throw any spanners in the works. But I won't be relaxing until the month is up. She's an unknown quantity.'

'What has she been doing while you've been working with Gillian?'

'Watching television. She asked me how I felt things went after the first evening, but hasn't enquired since. She seems mildly amused, but other than that totally disinterested.'

'Has Gillian commented at all on how she feels?' Maria asked. 'Has she had any insights? Made any disclosures?'

'No, but then I haven't pushed her. As I understand what we're doing, I'm a facilitator and she's doing the work herself. I know Gillian. If she has anything to say, she'll say it. You've also got to remember that Libby is there all the time. I reckon the poor kid is as nervous of her as I am. The last time I made any real progress Libby ran off, taking Gillian halfway around the country to get her away from me. Why she's enabling us to do this work is more than likely for some perverse reason of her own. I'm just praying that we can get the job done before she blows, and that we'll have laid a firm enough foundation so that when the powder-keg goes off, Gillian can withstand it.'

Both women nodded. There was nothing much else to say.

'Well done, both of you.' Gráinne smiled, raising her glass to Maria and me. 'We may be on the road to truly changing this girl's life. Now, let's eat.'

'Amen to that,' I said.

The date for the case review I had called for Connie Kelly fell in the middle of the month I was doing the regression work with Gillian. A review is a meeting of all professionals involved in a particular case, and the purpose of it is to assess whether or not that child's needs are being met as efficiently as they could be. The young person who is the subject of the review, and his/her parents, if they are still living and can be contacted, are invited and are encouraged to participate fully in the discussion. The days where all decisions are made behind the family's back are long since gone, thankfully. This being the case, a meeting with the Kellys in attendance had the potential to be at the very least an interesting affair, and I was far from as focused as I should have been.

The meeting was held in the conference room in our offices. The week before, I made another visit to the file room and took more detailed notes. I wrote a report outlining all the events that had led me to have such serious concerns for Connie. I considered including my meeting with Selina Canning, but decided against it. As Josephine had so concisely put it, I had no evidence. I just hoped that the bare facts of Connie's story would convince the assembled professionals that there was real cause for alarm.

My other concern (and it was a concern because I knew I was going to be asked) was: what exactly did I want from the review? Connie was no more ready to be placed in care than Gillian was, and anyway I had promised her that I would not go down that road. I was seeing her twice a week at the health centre, and although I was extremely dissatisfied at how little progress I was making, I *was* meeting her regularly and without any interference. As I thought about the case, something suddenly occurred to me: I had visited Connie countless times. I had also been with her parents and the rest of her family on a number of occasions. But I had never encountered them all together. *I had never seen Connie with her parents!* Thinking back on my visits to the Kelly home, I realised that I almost always had to cut them short due to the levels of violence or insanity.

Which was, of course, why I had booked the room in the health centre for my homework sessions with Connie.

Perhaps, I thought, if I could get Connie at home, I would see something that I had missed. What was her body language like around her parents? How did they react to her? The Kellys had always made any visits so unpleasant that I rarely went to see them – but perhaps that was their intention. I decided that the most sensible course of action was to ask the review board to seek a Supervision Order for Connie. This meant that the court would issue a writ insisting that Connie's parents allow health board staff to see her, in the family home if need be and on a regular basis, even if they visited every day.

The review went better than I had expected. The professionals met first, each delivering their reports on how the Kellys had been over the past twelve months. Josephine chaired the meeting. We heard from the family psychiatrist, from Connie's principal (Ms Duff had decided not to attend), from Sinéad, who was still peripherally involved in the case, and finally I was asked to give my report. It had the desired effect. The group was amazed and slightly uncomfortable. Why had no one heard these details before? Eventually Dr Maloney, the psychiatrist, spoke up and voiced the question that was on everyone's lips.

'This is . . . this is very distressing. Can I ask you, Mr Dunphy, where did you get this information?'

'It's in some old files,' Sinéad said, and I wondered if I heard a slight edge to her voice.

'Old files?'

'I wasn't making any progress with Connie, wasn't learning anything. So, since I couldn't think of anything else to do, I looked back through the records on the family. It's all there, Doctor. It hasn't been hidden away.'

'Well, we must do something, I think.'

'What would you propose, Doctor?' Josephine asked.

I could tell she wasn't happy with the way the review was going, but I didn't know why.

'Well, this young man seems to have been the primary worker. Let's hear what he has to say. What do you feel would be the best course of action, Mr Dunphy?'

'I want us to apply for a Supervision Order.'

'Could we ever stand over it?' Josephine asked 'The house is an extremely volatile environment.'

'That's what they want us to think, Jo. You've heard the reports here today. Mr and Mrs Kelly are more or less at equilibrium. Why is it that they always seem to have an episode when one of us is there? I think it's because they're hiding something, and don't want us around.'

'I'm not sure if that's true, but they are most certainly not a serious risk at the moment,' Dr Maloney said. 'Why don't we get them in here and see what they have to say?'

Mr and Mrs Kelly were scarcely recognisable. They were clean, well-groomed and smartly dressed. They were introduced to everyone, and each of us gave a summarised and de-jargonised account of what had been said. The Kellys said very little during this, except to explain that Connie had chosen not to attend and to ask Dr Maloney a few questions. They seemed to be very anxious to please him and he in turn was polite and pleasant with them. I sensed that there was a genuine fondness there, and I was glad. It was good that at least *one* of the professionals involved had some affection for them. They were a difficult and unloved couple, and perhaps that had contributed to the problems they had experienced.

When each of us had spoken, Josephine broached the issue of the Supervision Order. In fairness to her, she said that the request was coming from the group – it would have been easy to blame me, but she didn't. The Kellys looked at her blankly. They didn't know what a Supervision Order was.

'This means that, if the Order is granted, the judge would say that a health board person, Shane there for example, would have to come and see Connie on a regular basis, and that when he came, you would have to let him into the house and not make life difficult for him when he got there.'

We all waited for their response. For a moment it seemed that they were still uncertain as to what we were talking about. Then Mrs Kelly started wailing. Her face did not crumple like other people's do when they start crying; she just opened her mouth and noise came out. She also began to rock. As she did so the table we were all sitting around thumped and thudded on the floor as her gut rebounded off its edge where she sat. Mr Kelly continued to sit next to her, smiling benignly at everyone. The review meeting was over. If anyone had been in doubt about the need for a Supervision Order, they were not any more. Despite themselves, the Kellys had made my point for me.

After the meeting, I decided to act on a hunch, one that I hoped would further enlighten me as to what was really going on with Connie.

I parked my car half a mile up the road from the estate, just inside a narrow laneway and out of sight from the road, and then walked the distance to the horseshoe of houses. But I didn't go to the Kelly house. I went right across the road and knocked on the door of a little bungalow.

Mrs Jones was a tiny woman, stooped with age and almost bald. She leaned on her walking stick and squinted up at me in the waning evening light, and I saw that she had a wispy beard of white hair. I was reminded of Yoda, from the *Star Wars* movies.

'What?' she asked, peering at me, looking puzzled.

'Mrs Jones, I'm a friend of Connie's. Can I step in for a moment?'

A look of panic spread across her face and she peered around me at number 8.

'No! You have to go! I know who you are, and you have to go. If they see you here, I'll be in trouble. They won't care that I'm an old woman. That won't matter to *them*. Now go away. Shoo!'

'Mrs Jones, no one knows I'm here. Mr and Mrs Kelly are in town, and I know that Mick is away having tests done. You are completely safe.'

She glanced about suspiciously and then beckoned me in, closing the door quickly and shuffling down the hall to the kitchen. She sat on a kitchen chair and looked at me expectantly.

'What do you want with me?'

'Connie tells me you've been very good to her.'

'Yes. That's not a crime, is it?'

'I'm not a policeman, Mrs Jones.'

'She is a sweet child who has suffered. My own children are long gone. I'm alone in this vale of tears. She is company for me – and she's safe here.'

'Safe from what? How has she suffered?'

'You won't get that from me. Enough to say she comes and sleeps here and she knows her rest will not be disturbed.'

'She comes every night?'

'She has not slept in that house for three years now.'

'I didn't know that.'

'Well, you do now. You must go. I have nothing further to tell you. You leave me alone now.'

'What's going on over there, Mrs Jones? I want to help her – I want to stop it, whatever it is. If you tell me, I can do something about it.'

'You are a foolish young man. You will only make things worse, worse for all of us. We have ways of doing things, around here, that you would not understand. She's safe with me.'

'Not all the time. Where is she now?'

'She's all right.'

'Is she here?'

Something flitted across her eyes. It was only a tiny movement, but I caught it. She had shown me straight into the kitchen. I didn't know how many rooms were in these little houses, but there were at least three more than the one we were in. I figured that Connie was either in the living room or the bedroom. I decided not to push her on it.

'Will you tell her something for me, Mrs Jones? Tell her I only want what's best for her. I know that bad things have happened to her, and probably still are happening from time to time. If she'll just talk to me . . . I want to help.'

Mrs Jones remained impassive on her chair. I had no idea whether or not I had made any impression on her.

'I'll see myself out.'

I moved as quickly as I could to the road so that none of the neighbours could get a good look at me. I stopped to light a cigarette, and as I did I glanced back at the bungalow. The edge of one of the curtains was pulled back for a second as someone looked out. I flicked the lid of my Zippo closed and put it back in my pocket, gazing at that window. Was it Connie?

If it was, she'd heard what I had said. Maybe it would make a difference. Maybe.

I started back towards my car. When I got there, one of my tyres was flat, with a long slash right through to the tube. Someone had spotted me, after all, and wanted to let me know. I looked around the hedges and ditches to see if I could spy anyone. If the culprit was there, that person silently watched me change the wheel, listening as I cursed loudly and colourfully.

I rang Father Dashiell, the McCoy's parish priest.

'No one has seen Max in several weeks', he said.

'Father, it's imperative that I speak to him. I've managed to secure a place for him in the detox centre again. Their conditions are that he *must* make contact with them himself and convince them that he's a willing participant. Do you have a key to his house?'

'No. I don't know anyone who has a spare. He is a very private man. I have no idea whether or not he is at his house, or has gone back to England. I would think that some delicate questioning at the local off-licence may bear some fruit. I believe – I believe that he is at his lowest ebb, at the moment. The loss of his children has been a sore trial.'

'I understand that. It was necessary, Father. If there had been another way . . .'

'Of course. I hope you find him. He needs all the help he can get.'

'I'll find him.'

I borrowed Francesca's car. She had never worked with Max, and he wouldn't know the car as a health board vehicle. At eleven o'clock on a Tuesday morning I did as the good Father had suggested and stopped off at the local off-licence. They saw Max almost daily. That meant, as I had suspected, that he was holed up in the house.

All the curtains were drawn. The window through which Victor had climbed had been repaired. I parked slightly up the road, turned off the engine, and waited. I had brought along some sandwiches, a flask of coffee and I had all the time in the world.

Two hours later the sandwiches were eaten, the coffee was drunk, I was bursting to go to the toilet and I was bored out of my mind. I had a book in the back, but I was afraid to read it in case I missed Max when he came out. For the same reason, I was unwilling to nip down the road to the nearest pub to use the toilet.

An hour and a half later, I decided To hell with it! and went into the pub, buying a box of cigarettes while I was there. I reasoned that he had to walk past the pub to get to the off-licence, so I would see him on the way back. Feeling somewhat relieved but somewhat ineffective, I returned to my post.

At eight o'clock that night, Max walked stiffly out of his front door. He looked utterly wretched, a scraggy, unkempt beard that was more neglect than design covering his chin, a filthy pair of jeans hanging off his arse and a jumper that looked like it had not seen a washing machine in many months about his torso. He turned right at the gate and walked towards town. I let him get a good distance ahead, and then drove past him, keeping him in sight in the rear-view mirror. I parked across from the off-licence and waited. Max had to go this way, so if he was, in fact, shopping for bread or milk, I would see him going into the corner shop as opposed to the liquor store. Unfortunately, groceries were not his target this evening, and he turned into the off-licence as expected. I got out of the car and followed him in.

He had, apparently, not spent much time browsing the shelves, because when I went in he was already at the counter, a bottle of bargain-bin vodka being put into a brown paper bag for him. I waited for him to turn and see me. His eyes met mine, but he did not say hello, and pushed past me on to the street. I followed him and grabbed his shoulder.

'Jesus Christ, Max, will you talk to me?'

He shook loose of my grip and shoved me in the chest with all his strength. I was not expecting the blow, and staggered back a few steps. He didn't stop there, and came after me, angry now, and swinging at me with his left. I hunched up and took the punch on my shoulder, then stepped aside as his momentum carried him off balance. He fell against the wall.

'You finished?' I asked him.

He was breathing heavily, the exertion having been too much for him.

'Leave me alone, you bastard.'

'No.'

'Leave me alone!' he shouted and launched himself at me again, ramming into my body with his head. I was ready this time and caught him by his shoulders and pushed him back. He sat down hard on the pavement.

'Now you listen to me, you arsehole. We are going to talk. I've waited all fucking day for you to surface, and I'm not leaving until you hear what I've got to say.'

'Say it then, you cunt, and let me go home.'

I held out my hand and he took it and I pulled him to his feet. Now that I could see him close up, he looked even worse. The whites of his eyes were yellowed. He had aged, his face was leathery and lined, and he had lost a good deal of weight. It made me afraid for him. He was sick and getting sicker.

'The de-tox centre will take you again. I've got their number here. They want you to ring them to set up a date for going in. You can call them from my phone.'

'Is that all?'

'Yeah.'

'Okay. I'll be seeing you.'

He shuffled past me and began to walk down the street back towards his house. I ran after him.

'Max, what the fuck is wrong with you? This will help you to kick the booze! Don't you want to get the kids back? Isn't this what you've been waiting for?'

He stopped and looked at me, and I saw that he was crying.

'You stupid, pretentious do-gooder *prick*. Don't you see? I've been here before. I've done it. Didn't work. I came out and the need for a drink was like a fire in my gut. I went straight to the pub as soon as I got off the bus. I managed to keep it hidden for a while, but it soon got out of control, just like it always does. Now you tell me, you fucker, why I should waste my time going in there again? What difference will it make?'

'You want to make it work. You told me you did . . .'

'I said that before, too. But you see, I say these things, and I even mean them for a while. And then *this* starts calling to me. And I can't refuse it. It owns me.'

He brandished the bottle at me, and screwed the lid off and took a long, sucking gulp. I grimaced as I imagined the foul stuff burning its way down his throat.

'So you see, it's over. You can take your de-tox bullshit and shove it right up your arse as far as you can get it.'

'What do you want me to tell Cordelia and Victor and Ibar?'

The fight went out of him then, and he took another throatful of vodka, tears streaming down his face.

'Tell them I just couldn't do it any more. Tell them I'm sorry.'

'Max . . .'

'No. No more. I can't. It hurts too much.'

I reached out to him, imploring him to stay and talk to me, but he shook his head and lurched away. He staggered off up the road, clutching the only thing in his life that mattered, wrapped in a brown paper bag. I stood there watching him go, suddenly realising that I was crying too.

PART THREE

Pictures of Spiderweb

For you took what's before me
And what's behind me
Took right and left and all around me
You took my name
And you took my station
And God as well, if I'm not mistaken

Dònal Òg, Anonymous
(8th century bardic poem)

10

I was in the Indian restaurant with Andi and Muriel, celebrating. The next day I was going to court with Josephine and Sinéad to seek the Supervision Order for Connie. While things were otherwise at a standstill with her, I felt that this was a significantly positive development. Josephine was confident that the Order would be granted. Although her attitude towards me since the review had been a little frosty, Sinéad had agreed to take a more active part in the case and had helped me to do some work with Mr and Mrs Kelly to prepare them for our more constant presence. I felt that maybe, once we began working in the home, we would see some concrete progress. I knew that Sinéad was angry about my report, which, as Josephine had pointed out, suggested the Kellys had been left to rot by previous workers. I was upset that she should feel that way, but it was a small enough sacrifice to make if it meant that we could do something real for the Kellys.

I raised my bottle of Tiger beer.

'To the Irish legal system. May it, for once, not perform like an ass.'

Andi and Muriel cheered and clinked bottle necks.

Muriel was a slim, dark-haired girl with glasses and a similar dress-sense to her girlfriend.

'It truly depends on the judge you get, of course,' she said, picking at her lamb rogan josh.

'Really? I thought this was just an open-and-shut kind of thing. A formality.'

'It should be, but we've both seen cases that should have been a doddle turn into shit-storms, haven't we?' Andi said to Muriel.

I had chicken sagwaala. The food in the restaurant was actually pretty good, despite Andi's initial joking about it. We had taken to coming here on special occasions. The staff were polite, the seating was comfortable and it was never difficult to get a table.

'Do you remember the Connors case?' Muriel said.

'Tell him about it, Muriel. You'll love this, Shane.'

Muriel smiled and put down her fork. She tore off a piece of naan bread and picked crumbs off it as she spoke.

'I had a family at the refuge. Mum and two kids. The father kept on coming around, hanging about outside trying to intimidate them. We'd call the police, but there was little they could do. He was standing a small distance away, not acting threateningly, in a public car park. They sympathised, but that was about it. So, we decided to apply for a barring order. The details were fairly straightforward. He was an alcoholic and a drug abuser. He also pushed. There was every class of low-life coming in and out of the family home at all hours of the day and night. When the woman asked him to take his business elsewhere, he beat the shit out of her and threw her and the children out of the house. Now, you'd imagine that this would be a classic example of going in, presenting the evidence, getting your order, thank you very much judge, let's all go home for tea.'

'But I assume it wasn't?'

'The judge was new, one of those visiting ones that come when the usual guy is off playing golf or something. We also had a young lawyer. Our usual, Trudy, was on leave. I started to realise that we were in trouble when he wanted to know if this was your man's first offence. Now, gobshite had a rap-sheet as long as your arm, but it was all drug-related. He had never been up for domestic violence before. So the judge decides that he will not, in this instance, grant the order. He recommends that they go to *marriage guidance counselling*, and asks to see them in a month to review the situation.'

'And I suppose that this was not helpful under the circumstances?'

'He beat this girl to within an inch of her life,' Andi said, shaking her head at the recollection. 'She needed reconstructive surgery, for fuck's sake. She was afraid to be on the same street as him. No, marriage guidance counselling was not an option. Of course baby lawyer just stands there with his fucking gob hanging open and decides not to point any of this out to our wise and learned judge.'

'So what did you do?'

'Well, we couldn't use the law to achieve our end,' Muriel said. 'So we decided to step outside of it. Here we had a drug dealer from out of town, hanging around and making himself visible. I began to wonder what the other dealers would think about that.'

'You didn't!'

'I did. I made a couple of phone calls, and spoke to some people I know, and just put it out there on the grapevine that this guy was looking to expand his turf. Which he may have been doing, for all I know.'

'What happened?'

'Let's just say he stopped hanging around outside the refuge fairly quickly.'

'So you're basically telling me that it ain't over until the fat man in the black robes sings.'

'Precisely.'

'I'll keep it in mind, but I don't see how this can go wrong tomorrow. I've got a good feeling in my gut.'

I thought I was going to die.

My insides seemed hell-bent on making their way up my throat and into the toilet bowl. My bowels were one minute shrivelling up to the size of walnuts and then expanding and inflating at an alarming rate. My large and small intestines felt like they were wrestling with one another, and I wasn't sure which one was winning. I was bathed in sweat and freezing all at the same time. I was also supposed to be in court and I couldn't get to my phone for fear of spraying substances from orifices as yet undetermined all over my living room. I eventually dragged myself on all fours over to the coffee table upon which I had dumped my phone the previous night. Andi's number was the first one in my phone, and I couldn't focus on trying to make my way to J to find Josephine's.

'Hey Shane. What's the crack?'

'Andi, I'm supposed to be in court.'

'I know.'

'I think I have food poisoning.'

'Couldn't have. Me and Muriel are grand.'

'I'm really sick. Can you get hold of Jo and explain for me?'

'Ring her yourself.'

'Andi, I can't. I have to go. I'm gonna be sick.'

'Enjoy.'

I made it back to the toilet – barely.

Owing to my absence, the case was adjourned for a month. To say that Josephine was angry with me would be an understatement. I knew that I deserved her ire – she had had her phone switched off, since she was in court, and had not received Andi's call until midday; to all intents and purposes, I had simply not turned up to a court hearing – so I stood in her office and absorbed the flow of invective with my head bowed. After five minutes or so, she ran out of steam.

'Are you feeling better?'

'Haven't got much of an appetite, but I can drink water and hold it down.'

'Shane, that was *almost* a rhetorical question. You're standing in my fucking office, so the appropriate answer is: "Yes, I'm fine." I'm still too annoyed at you to be interested in a blow by blow account of how your goddam digestive tract is doing. Now get out and go and do whatever you have to do. If you *ever* let me down like that again, I will not be responsible for my actions.'

'Okay. I can only apologise again—'

'Get – out!'

One month later, Josephine, Sinéad and I were seated in court, waiting to be seen by the judge. In the Family Court, cases are heard *in camera*, meaning that each case is seen in private. Our lawyer, Gloria, was dealing with several cases that morning, so we took a seat among the other groups seeking justice and waited. After two hours we were ushered into the judge's chambers and Gloria spoke for a few moments in legalese.

The judge was a corpulent man with a florid face and not much hair. He listened closely and then turned his rheumy gaze upon us.

'You are applying for a Supervision Order for one Veronica Kelly, of 8, Douglas Terrace. I believe that you have some reports to support your application?'

Jospehine nodded at Sinéad, who without pause launched into her brief report. She had not had much contact with the family over the time I had been working with them, but she gave the main points of the case articulately and concisely. I had a copy of the report I had given at the case review, and stood beside her, waiting to relate my own perspective, which I modestly felt would be even more valuable. Sinéad concluded after around two minutes.

'We also have a report from the community child-care worker, who has been the main worker on the case over the past seven months.'

'Yes, yes, I don't think that will be necessary. Are you both in concurrence that this is in the best interests of the child?' the judge asked Josephine and Sinéad.

'We are.'

'So be it. The order is granted as of this date.'

I felt like I had just been kicked in the genitals. I did not, it seemed, even warrant a short input into the discussions. I was delighted that the order had been granted, but devastated at my treatment. I stood, slightly behind the two social workers, and rolled my report into a ball. There was some further debate, none of which I heard. I was only aware of a muted thudding in my head and a sense of having been cast aside like so much garbage. What killed me the most was that I was fully aware I was being childish. Connie was now under a Supervision Order, which was what we had set out to achieve. My ego was of no importance. Knowing this, however, was of no help. I dropped the crumpled report in the wastebasket on the way out. It seemed that was all it was worth.

*

Libby opened the front door, smiling at me warmly. I immediately knew that the moment I had been waiting for had arrived. Whatever she had been planning either had been, or was about to be, put into action. I gritted my teeth and smiled back.

'Hey, Libby. Gillian ready to do some work today?'

'Oh, she's ready all right. She's waiting for you in the therapy room.'

The words 'therapy room' were virtually dripping with sarcasm.

'That's great, Libby. Sure I'll go right on through, so.'

'You do that, Shaney-boy.'

The door to the room was closed. Libby stood halfway down the living area and folded her arms, waiting for me to go inside. I was tense now, knowing that something was going to happen, and the chances of it being in any way pleasant were negligible. I looked back at her.

'What are you waiting for?' she taunted.

I felt a trickle of sweat roll down the small of my back, and grasped the doorknob. I could sense Libby's excitement. I turned the knob and swung the door open.

The snarl of the dog that was waiting for me in the room sounded like a klaxon and I threw myself backwards as it lunged for me. I landed with a sickening thud right onto my coccyx and a current of pain shot up into my lower back. *Christ, that is going to have one hell of a bruise on it tomorrow*, I thought briefly, but then I was scrabbling to get purchase on the threadbare carpet with the heels of my boots, trying to shove myself as far as I could away from the animal. My back hit the wall and I could go no farther. The dog stopped in the doorway of the room and remained there, growling at me. When it saw that I was subdued, it turned tail and padded back to a large pile of fabric in the centre of the room, which it climbed on top of and settled down upon. Laughter brought me back to my senses and I turned to see Libby and Gillian together, almost hysterical in their mirth. Gillian must have been in one of the bedrooms all along. I pulled myself up and walked stiffly back to them.

'Very funny,' I said, finding it difficult not to get really angry. I was in pain, I had received a nasty shock, and I was also disappointed. The work with Gillian had been going well, and I had hoped that we would be able to complete it. We almost had, too, but were three sessions away from the final regression – a very delicate juncture. Gillian had been exploring what it felt like to be a member of her family, what that meant to her, and had been trying to identify her place and role. This particular piece of personal development was pivotal for her being able to make the break from her mother and move into care – Libby had timed the strike very well.

I looked back into the therapy room. The 'nest' upon which the dog was sitting was made up of the tent and the duvets and blankets, all piled into a heap. I felt an even more concentrated surge of annoyance.

Libby had not done this unthinkingly. She was telling me exactly what she thought of the work we had been doing.

'Doesn't Rex look cosy in there?' Libby sneered from behind me.

Rex was her favourite, the one the neighbours said she was intimate with.

'He looks extremely comfortable, Libby. I don't suppose you could have waited for us to finish what we were doing before you moved him in.'

'Ah, ye'd done enough! All that navel-gazing isn't good for you. My Gillian told me she was sick of it. She just didn't want to hurt your feelings. Isn't that right, Gill?'

'That's right, Mammy. He gets soppy when he's upset.'

I shook my head and gazed at the huge animal perched atop the tools I had been working with for the past four weeks. There was something deeply symbolic about what I was looking at, something archetypal, as Jung would have put it. The scene was like something from a Greek tragedy, the dog like some mythological beast, standing guard over the gateway into Gillian's subconscious. Perhaps Libby *had* been paying attention. The thought made it almost more horrifying.

'Well, I suppose there's no point in my sticking around today.'

'No. You be off with yourself. I've got my room, and this is exactly what I wanted it for. You've had your fun with Gillian, but that's enough of that. Everyone's happy.'

I ignored Libby, feeling too angry to deal with her now.

'I'll see you later in the week, Gillian. I'll pick you up from school.'

'No! I don't want to see you any more.'

I sighed and walked to the door.

'Yeah. I've heard that one before.'

I don't know if Libby stayed by the door as I walked to the car, but the dogs made no move towards me. Maybe they sensed that in my present mood I was as much a danger to them as they were to me.

My mobile phone rang on the way into work two weeks later. I was deep in thought as I drove. Gillian had disappeared again after she and her mother had destroyed the room. There had been no contact, no word from the school, and a ring around the refuges had revealed nothing. This was to the fore of my mind as I reached for the hand-set and looked quickly at the display. The word 'OFFICE' was blinking there. I pressed the answer key and put the phone to my ear.

'Yeah.'

'Shane, where are you?'

It was Josephine.

'I'm on my way to the office. It's only nine fifteen. I'm not late, am I?'

'No, no, it's not that. I've some bad news.'

'What?'

I wasn't even worried. I figured it was something trivial. I don't know why I wasn't more concerned, I just wasn't.

'Max McCoy was found dead last night.'

I felt my mind struggle to process the information.

'Are you sure?'

'No mistake. He was found by a girlfriend. She had a key to his house, apparently.'

'I didn't even know he was seeing anyone.'

'Well, it seems he was. She let herself in and found him in the bedroom. He had taken an overdose.'

'Oh Jesus.'

'Are you okay?'

'Yeah . . . yeah, I'm all right. The children . . .'

'They haven't been told.'

'Does Dympna know?'

'Yes, but they're waiting for you to get out there. The kids will go to school as normal, and you can see them this evening.'

'I'll be with you in ten minutes.'

'Okay. Are you sure you're all right?'

'Yeah. I'll see you in a bit.'

I put the phone in my pocket. At that moment, all I could feel was a creeping numbness. Could I have done anything to prevent this turn of events? I felt that I had tried as hard as I could to help Max. I had extended the hand of friendship. Could I have allowed access to continue, despite his intoxication and the effect it was having on the children? That was a question I would never have the answer to now. I wanted to press the accelerator to the floor and just get into the office. I needed to be busy, doing something. I felt trapped and impotent in the car. I would, of course, be no use to anyone if I drove my car into a ditch. I turned on the stereo, thinking that some music might calm me. I had a Leonard Cohen CD with me that morning. Normally I loved Leonard Cohen, but I should have realised that in the circumstances he wasn't going to lift my mood. I switched it off again and just drove.

Josephine met me at reception and we went up to her office. We sat and looked at each other for a moment, unsure where to start.

'What happened?' I asked. 'Tell me from the beginning.'

Josephine reached for a page of scribbled notes.

'I don't have a lot of information. The ambulance services received a call through 999 at around ten forty-five last night. They went to the address of Max McCoy, where he was found in bed. He had consumed a dangerous amount of vodka and a large number of tranquillisers, which he had on prescription. He was given some treatment on the scene and then brought to hospital, where he was declared dead at twelve ten in the morning of liver failure brought about by a massive overdose of the aforementioned drugs, although apparently cirrhosis would have done the job very soon anyway. We can't tell the family any definite cause of death until the coroner has been over him. The woman who made the call is one Wendy Tremaine. She lives just outside the village and has been seeing Max, so she says, off and on for twelve months. They met at an AA meeting. She was at the scene and let the medics in. I was contacted by Penelope Granger, the hospital social worker, this morning at eight thirty. She recognised Max's name as one of ours, and rang out of courtesy. I called Dympna, then you. That's what I know.'

I heaved a deep sigh. The similarities between the cause of death of Beatrice McCoy and her husband were too close for comfort.

'What will happen to the children now?' I asked.

'Dympna was doing us a favour in the short term. She never intended to have the children permanently. I suppose they'll go into care. Residential or long-term foster. Wherever we can place them.'

'I really don't want these kids placed in res. They'd be eaten up by it.'

'Give me a viable alternative.'

'Leave it with me.'

'We'll get maybe another couple of months out of Dympna, but after that we'll be under serious pressure to have them moved,' Josephine said. 'I don't want to take advantage of that woman. She's not even really a foster parent, you know. She's a friend of the family who has stepped in to help out.'

'I know that. Just give me a few days to talk to Fostering and see what we can do. The kids will want to know when I talk to them. Maybe not tonight, but they'll start wondering as soon as the shock wears off.'

'Absolutely. How are you feeling?'

'Like shit.'

'I don't want you getting all cut up over this now, d'you hear me? It was unavoidable. You've pulled out all the stops for the McCoys, gone above and beyond the call of duty. Max was on a self-destruct course before you ever came on the scene, so there's no point in blaming yourself. He was a decent man who went astray somewhere along the line. You did all you could.'

'I hope so, Josephine.'

'You know you did.'

'It doesn't feel like that just now.'

'You've just had the legs kicked out from underneath you. You're bound to be disoriented.'

'Is that what it is?'

'You've never lost a client before, have you?'

The question seemed almost absurd. It had never occurred to me that things like this could happen in social care, but then, why wouldn't they? I was working with people under the most extreme stress and unhappiness. Of course it was a possibility – I had simply never countenanced it before.

'Not like this.'

'It happens from time to time. It always feels like the end of the world. You'll get over it.'

'Maybe I shouldn't "get over it". A man is dead.'

'You have to get over it. The children need you.

The team here needs you. As horrible as it sounds under the present circumstances: life goes on.'

My Adam's apple felt too big and my eyes felt wet. I rubbed at them and cleared my throat.

'You're right. I just need some time. I'll be fine by this evening. Listen, I have to go and talk to Fostering; see what we can do.'

Josephine nodded and reached out a hand. I took it and she held mine gently.

'You come and talk to me if this gets on top of you. We have counsellors, you know, if you need something more in-depth. But if you need a friend . . . you know where I am.'

'Thanks, Jo. I know that.'

'Good. Now go on,' she said, grinning at me. 'I've got a ton of work to do.'

I sat outside Dympna's house for ten minutes, trying to work out the best way to tell the children. I had always heard policemen and doctors say that this was the toughest part of their jobs, telling families that their loved ones were gone, but it wasn't something I had ever really considered having to do myself. After ten minutes, I hadn't come up with anything that didn't sound brutal and devastating, and decided that that was because the news *was* brutal and devastating no matter how you dressed it up. I got out of the car and went inside.

Dympna showed me into a lounge that I had never been in before, and came back with the three children.

Victor and Ibar were their usual detached selves, Victor grinning lopsidedly at me and giving me an awkward wave as he came in. Cordelia knew there was something up. Her expression was half sulky and half nervy. The three of them lined up on a large chaise-longue opposite me. I looked at them, and a sense of almost overwhelming panic swept over me. I had to fight the desire to get up and run out of the room. I gripped my knees tightly and gritted my teeth until it passed.

'What's up, Shane?' Cordelia asked, perplexed.

'I'm afraid I have some bad news,' I said, realising as I was saying it that it sounded trite and clichéd, but I just couldn't think of anything else to say. 'Max – your dad – became ill late last night. He was brought to hospital and they tried to help him but . . . it was too late. Too late to do anything. He died at around midnight. I'm so, so sorry.'

Ibar was sitting on the floor fiddling with the buckle on his shoe, and if he had heard or understood any of what I had said, he showed no sign of it. Victor and Cordelia gazed at me open-mouthed. Victor made a choking sound and stood up, clenching and unclenching his hands and looking around the room as if for something to latch onto that would help make sense of what he had just been told. Cordelia just continued to look at me in horror. Dympna placed a hand on Victor and pulled him back on to the couch, hugging and shushing him gently as tears claimed him.

'How . . . how did he die?' Cordelia asked.

'I don't really know. There will have to be a coroner's report. We won't know for sure until then.'

'Come on, Shane! You must know. Was it drink?'

'The alcohol had made him sick, but they don't know if that's what killed him. I'm sorry, Cordelia. I just don't have an answer for you.'

'He probably killed himself!' she said, anger invading her voice now and rising rapidly. 'I always knew that it would end up like this! Ever since Mummy died, I knew he'd leave us! How could he? How could he do this to us? We're only children. Why couldn't he be a daddy like everyone else's? Why couldn't he have loved us?'

Dympna reached out to her but Cordelia shook her off and stood up. She walked over to me and knelt down in front of me, grasping me by both arms, shaking me, not roughly, but as a way of expressing the urgency she felt.

'What are we going to do now, Shane?' she asked, almost shouting, tears of anger and fear coursing down her cheeks. 'What the hell are we going to do?'

I knew that I was crying too and made no attempt to stop myself. I had no words to comfort her. I had not lost both parents, was not an orphan and had never been adrift and alone in the world. There was nothing to say.

'Answer me!' she shouted, still shaking me. 'Why won't you answer me?'

'I can't!' I blurted, taking her wrists and pulling her

to me. 'I can't bring him back and I can't change what's happened. I'm sorry!'

She fought me for a moment and then collapsed onto me, her body racked with sobs.

'I can only tell you that I am *here*. We'll come through this. You love him. That won't ever change. Every time you think of him, just like every time you think of your mum, you'll feel sad. But it'll get less and less until you wake up one morning and you won't feel as sad any more. And right now, you've got Dympna, and you've got me. I'm just a phone call away any time you need me.'

I felt a tap on my shoulder.

Little Ibar stood beside Cordelia and me, his eyes red with crying and such pain etched on his face that I thought my heart would break. I had never seen him express any emotion at all other than bemusement – and now this.

'Daddy?' he said in a tiny voice.

Cordelia took him into her arms. I held them both and we stayed there like that.

'I'd like to tell you they'll be fine,' Dympna said as I was leaving. 'But this time, I'm not so sure. My God, Shane. I know that I should have seen this coming. But I didn't. I'm flabbergasted.'

'Me too,' I said.

My throat felt raw with crying and my chest felt hollow. I was all used up, and I knew it. Dympna squeezed my arm and smiled sadly at me.

'You take care. I'll see you tomorrow?'

'Yeah. Keep them home from school. I'll be over in the morning.'

'Okay. Drive safely.'

I went back to the office. I didn't know why – it was past going-home time and there would be nobody there but the cleaners. Maybe I didn't want to go back to my empty house with its dust and CDs and books and old furniture. Perhaps I didn't want my thoughts to catch up with me, and was afraid that if I stopped, they would and then there wouldn't be any going back. And there was, of course, the chance that I had no idea what I was doing and just ended up back there out of force of habit.

At any rate, at eight that evening I was seated at my desk, sipping a cup of black coffee and staring into space. I had my mail for the day in front of me, still lying unopened. I was suddenly very tired. Out of the corner of my eye, I noticed the red message light blinking on my phone. Absentmindedly I picked up the receiver and hit the button to play the recording. The computerised voice told me haltingly that the message had come in at three twelve that afternoon.

'Shane Dunphy,' said a husky female voice, 'I hope you are satisfied. You have blood on your hands as surely as if you stabbed Max McCoy through the heart. You are a murderer. All he needed was to be allowed see his children. All you had to do was stop being a bastard and say the word. If you hadn't been such a high and mighty power-freak, he'd be alive today. I hope you sleep well tonight knowing that you've orphaned those three children. Bye, bye now. I'll be seeing you.'

I listened to the message, then played it through once more.

The silence in the office mirrored the emptiness inside me.

Murderer.

Whoever she was, she had voiced what I had been thinking all day. I was to blame for this – I and no one else.

I hit the ERASE button so hard that the phone jumped. Then I hit it again and again and again. I continued to strike it, first with my finger and then with my fist, until the phone was a splintered pile of plastic and circuitry on my desk and the anger and self-pity subsided, leaving only a cold darkness that sought to consume me.

11

I looked at Connie as she worked. She was sitting at the long table in the room we used at the health centre, bent over her refill pad, working on a history essay. She looked tired and pinched, as if her sleep had not been restful in many nights. She looked up and caught me watching her.

'What?'

'Nothing. I was just thinking you look tired.'

'You don't look so hot yourself.'

'I *am* tired.'

'There you go, then. Takes one to know one.'

This type of interaction characterised all our conversations now. They were about nothing. I had started meeting her at the house, sometimes, but had learned nothing new. Mr and Mrs Kelly were sulky, but not purposefully obstructive and Mick just made himself scarce. The problem was that Connie was now even more unforthcoming than before. Out of stubbornness I had continued to see her on alternate visits in her home, but I was fully aware that it was a waste of time. Direct questions about Mrs Jones yielded only icy glares and silence. I was flat out of options, and I knew it. I had one last card to play, and I had decided I was going to play it that evening.

I had nothing to lose, and I was too worn out to think of anything else. It was make or break time.

I checked my watch.

'C'mon, Connie. Time to call it a day. I'll run you up home.'

She said nothing, but began packing her books and pens into her bag.

I drove into the estate, but instead of parking in front of the Kelly's house, I parked in front of Mrs Jones's. My previous call on her had taught me that discretion was wasted: if I tunnelled in I'd be seen by someone. I didn't talk to Connie, just got out and walked up to the front door of the bungalow. I didn't knock. I looked back and waited for her to make her decision. She was looking at me, then glancing nervously at her family home, as if waiting for her mother to explode out of the door at any moment, lumber across the green and rip her from the car. To be honest, I felt a little nervous too, so brazenly was I flouting the conventions of this strange place. Connie suddenly shot from the car and ran up beside me.

'What are you doing?' she asked me nervously, hopping from one foot to another in tension.

'We're going to have a chat with Mrs Jones. Together. We've played games for long enough, Connie. It's time to lay our cards on the table.'

I knocked on the door, three loud bangs.

'Please don't, Shane,' she said, her eyes pleading, wide with terror.

Suddenly I was convinced I had made a mistake. She wasn't ready for this. I would do more harm than good. I had messed up again. But then the door was opening and Mrs Jones was there, peering out at us from eyes that saw much more than anyone thought.

'You're back,' she said. 'Come to try again, have you?'

'Connie is with me,' I stuttered, very unsure how to proceed. My confidence was gone.

Connie ran past me and put her arm around the old woman's stooped shoulders.

'Do you want me to run him, Veronica? Eh?'

Connie looked at me, standing dejected on the doorstep, and then over at the dark windows of number eight. For a moment, she seemed about to tell Mrs Jones to send me away. Then her face changed.

'Let him come in. What harm can it do now?'

'If that's what you want,' Mrs Jones said, and the two shuffled down the hall ahead of me. I went in and closed the door.

Connie brought me into a gloomy sitting room, where the only light came from the bars of an electric fire. The curtains were closed and I felt like I was in a tomb. I sat on a low couch, the cushions of which were so loosely stuffed that I seemed to sink even deeper into them. Connie left and came back moments later with a tray and tea things. I smiled weakly at her and took the small china cup she offered. I heard movement in the gloom behind me and Mrs Jones hobbled in.

'Well, well, well. We have a visitor. Isn't that grand, Connie?'

'Maybe I was a bit hasty,' I said as the old women plonked herself down on an armchair in the corner.

She reached over and began to fiddle with an old radio that looked to be an antique. Suddenly music filled the room in a great gush of sound. She quickly turned the volume down so we could talk. I recognised the song by Count Basie's orchestra with Tony Bennett on vocals: 'I've Grown Accustomed to Her Face', a show-tune from *My Fair Lady*. Nice.

'Whether you were hasty or not, it seems to me that Connie must now decide what to do, mmm?'

'Yes.'

I sipped the black tea and looked at Connie, who was nibbling at a pink wafer biscuit and gazing wide-eyed at us through the darkness.

'Tell him,' she said, so quietly that I had to ask her to repeat it.

Mrs Jones nodded.

'All right, child. We'll tell him.'

And they began to speak, Connie first, then Mrs Jones, until it seemed that both voices became one and my head began to swim and it was like I was dreaming what they said, Connie's tale becoming my nightmare until I thought I would scream. But I did not, and the story unveiled itself before me like a picture made of a spider web.

'I don't remember when it began,' Connie said. 'In my mind, it was just always happening, as far back as my memories go. When I think hard, I can remember being in a bed with bars, like a cot, and a man coming. I don't know who he was, but that doesn't mean anything, because people often don't have faces in dreams. He comes and he . . . touches me. Puts things in me. Hurts me. Then he's gone. Most children remember their first day at school or a birthday party or a trip to the circus as their earliest memory. I remember him. The Man.

'As I grew up, Mick would come to my and Denise's room in the night, and wake us up and one or other of us would have to go to the shed with him. I don't know why he'd bring us out there, 'cause he had his own room. Maybe he didn't want to do it where he slept. We'd never know who it was going to be, and there was no pattern to it. He might take me for three nights running, then her for one, then me again for six, or I might not have to go with him for months on end. I hated it. It should never have happened and I knew it and he knew it and he knew I knew it. I'd fight him, and bite sometimes, but it made no difference. Once I bit it when he made me put it in my mouth, and he beat me so bad they had to bring me to the hospital. But it was worth it, to see the look on his face.

'They would have "visitors" over, sometimes. They would tell us that they were friends of Daddy's, or friends of Mick's. We'd never have seen them before, but we were supposed to be "nice" to them. You know what *that* meant. Sometimes they were all right – gentle with us, y'know what I'm saying? But sometimes they'd want to hurt us. One of them told me he wanted to hear me scream, and he kept hurting until he made me, even though I tried really hard not to. I didn't want to please him, the bastard.

'They'd give us stuff, from time to time, the visitors. Toys, sweets, but Mick or Daddy would always take them away. When I got a bit more sense, I realised that they were getting paid for letting these fellas have their time with us. But I didn't know that for a long time. I was too little.'

'I watched them coming and going in that house for years, the huge woman and her dark men,' Mrs Jones said. 'I've lived here all my life, and I know that there are bad people hereabouts, bad men, and I know what they do. I know their desires and their urges. That house became a beacon to them; they were drawn to it like moths to a flame. I saw the destruction of Connie's sisters and I was afraid to do anything. Once I hid young Geraldine when a car arrived, and the young man, Mick, came, and he kicked my door in and he hit me and took her back. He said if I interfered again, he'd kill me. I believed him, and I did nothing for a time, because I was old and weak. But even the old become angry, and anger can be a powerful ally. Anger and guile.

'I waited. There is a terrible madness in that family, almost as if the evil in them couldn't allow them to function any more, like it was rotting them from the inside. I saw as the two old ones and their son came more and more under its control, and then I gathered my courage and I paid them a visit. I was mortally afraid, but I knew that I had to act. They were all sick the day I went, babbling and gibbering like monkeys. I told them I wanted Connie to do some work for me, get things from the shops and suchlike, and that I was afraid in the house because of break-ins down the village and wanted her to stay overnight with me sometimes. I said that I'd give them a few bob from my pension the odd time to make up for it. They were so far gone that day, they would have agreed to anything. Connie began spending a lot of time at my house. When Mick came banging over a week later, I smiled and told him that sure, hadn't he given me permission to have her. You see, they all suffer from the sin of pride, too. They don't like remembering the episodes when they aren't in control. Don't like it at all. And so we became friends, young Veronica and I. But like you said, I couldn't protect her all the time. They still got to her.'

'They brought us on trips sometimes,' Connie said. 'Instead of the visitors coming to us, we'd be brought to them. A car would come and one or both of us would be put into it and we'd be taken somewhere and it would happen. When I started going to Mrs Jones, it happened less and less, because I made sure I was hardly ever there. It got so's I only slept at home if Mick was staying somewhere else, and Daddy was gone so mad he was only a danger to himself. But I suppose it must have been eating me up some way, because I was always in trouble. I would just get mad for no reason, and I'd hit people and shout at my teachers and I couldn't concentrate. I got moved from school to school, and the guards were at the house a lot because I robbed things in town every chance I got. They never charged me – I think they felt sorry for me. One day, when I was ten, I was going to get the bus home from school when I heard a shout, and there was Mick in a car with two other men. He told me to get in, so I did. There wouldn't have been any point in running away. They'd have caught me.

'They took me to a house and kept me there for a long time. I lost track of time. Night, day, it was all the same. Men and some women, all the time wanting . . . wanting me to do things. Bad things. Worse than usual. I don't remember much of it.

'Then Mick was there, and he told me that if I didn't get my act together and stop drawing attention to the family, this was how it could be. Not just now and again, but for good. This could be my life. And he meant it, every word. He made me learn a story to explain where I had been, and dropped me home. I was good after that. They never heard a peep out of me at school, and you'd be surprised how being scared focuses the mind. My work improved.

'It still happened after that. It didn't stop, but you see, we're getting too old for them now. That's how it works. Nobody told me, but I know. I worked it out. Geraldine told me that it stopped for her when she got to be like a woman, and Denise is like that, and I nearly am. It won't be long now. Y'see? It's not so bad, when you think about it.'

I thought I would vomit. A sheen of sweat beaded my forehead and I found the air too close to breathe in the room. It was worse than I had dared imagine. I wanted to scream, to run over to number eight, smash the door in and beat them all until they were nothing but a red mess.

Connie smiled at me. She actually smiled.

'So there's not really much to worry about.'

Mrs Jones nodded and gazed at me with those eyes that were too young for a woman of her years. I tried to stop myself from trembling, and wondered desperately what I was going to do.

I sat outside the O'Gorman house, staring at it. I had been calling several times a week since Gillian and Libby had gone again, but no matter how much I blew the horn, the place remained implacable and unresponsive except for the slavering of the hounds. It was late evening and there wasn't a light on in the place. Dusk had descended, but I felt the need to sit in vigil for some reason.

I believed that I had let Gillian down, that I had failed her. If she was in there, I wanted her to know that I hadn't given up on her. So I stayed, listening to the night-time sounds and feeling sorry for myself.

Things had gradually begun to fall apart and I was powerless to prevent their continued descent into dysfunction. I knew that I had lost all focus after Max McCoy's death. But, if I were honest with myself, it had started before that. I had become far too involved in the three 'big' cases on my books, to the utter detriment of the others I was supposed to be involved in. I told myself that I was directing my time according to greatest need, that I was prioritising, but I wasn't so sure any more. The children I dedicated myself to were the ones who had nobody else. The kids in residential care or in the youth project had many other workers to depend on. If I didn't see them for a few weeks, there would be plenty of other people to pick up the slack – that's what I told myself. But my absence from these other cases had become more and more constant and my superiors, as well as the other staff involved, were far from happy. I protested that I was spread too thinly, had many cases in crisis, that there were always flash fires that needed putting out. The problem was, I couldn't believe the excuses that night. I *wanted* the tougher cases, I craved the challenge. I needed to feel I was on the edge, flying by the seat of my pants.

But I had also, for whatever reason, come to care deeply for these children: for Connie, Gillian, Victor, Ibar and Cordelia. It had gone beyond professional detachment. They called to something deep inside me and I had no choice but to respond. I was at the point where I had to admit that it was having a negative effect on the rest of my life. I was going down and I was pulling everyone else down with me.

I had talked to Josephine about it – I'd had no choice, she had called me into her office and asked me what the hell was going on with me – and she had been characteristically supportive while giving me a proverbial kick up the arse at the same time. I needed, she told me, to wind up these cases as quickly as possible, and direct my attention back to the other less dramatic ones. And maybe I would benefit from that counselling we had discussed before. I baulked at this suggestion, my natural arrogance feeling that I would work it out for myself in the end.

The tip of my cigarette glowed red in the shadows, and somewhere in the night a fox barked, followed by the scream of a vixen. I pushed the self-indulgent thoughts aside and turned my attention back to the gloom-soaked building before me. There was only one thing for it: I had to get a look inside. The real challenge was: *how was I going to get past the Hounds of the Baskervilles?* I picked up my mobile phone and rang a number. I didn't know how to get past the mutts.

But I knew a man who did.

'You look awful.'

'Yeah. I know. Things've been . . . challenging . . . of late.'

'I worry about you young people. You need to take some time off. Have some fun. There's more to life than this, you know.'

'Soon. I'm planning on taking some time soon.'

'I hope so. I shall check.'

'I know you will.'

'This is what you want. It works. I used one myself when I was doing family casework across the water. You press this red button and it emits a sound, undetectable by the human ear, but quite unpleasant for our canine friends. They won't be able to come within twenty feet of you. You just need to make sure you have a full battery pack in it, because if it gives out while you're within range of the dogs you'll be in a bit of bother, won't you?'

'I'll make sure.'

'There has to be easier ways to make a living, don't you think?'

'You've been doing it for thirty years. You're not in any position to talk.'

'Ah yes, but I've learned from my mistakes, you see. I know when to shut off. I don't think you do.'

'I'll have to remind you to give me the recipe for that.'

'I think it's something you need to learn for yourself, Shane.'

'In that case the lessons have already started.'

'Make sure you pay attention. You *will* be tested later.'

The machine was as big as a paperback book and a deep grey. On one end was a torch, on the opposite a gauze covered dome. A red button was embedded into one side, a blue into the other. The blue was for the torch, the red for the dog-deterrent. I checked that the batteries were in place and stepped out of the car. The two dogs at the front of the house looked up, but made no move or sound. They were getting used to me by now and were less agitated at my presence. Of course, if I placed one step onto their territory, that would change rapidly. I walked past the posts that had not had a gate hitched to them in many years. The two dogs out front looked at me with what could only have been surprise (dog faces are sometimes hard to read) and stood up. I knew this was a warning. They were saying: 'Okay now. That's far enough.' I took another step. That was it. They immediately exploded into noise and motion. I raised the box and pressed the red button.

The result was not instantaneous. I thought that the dogs would yelp and fall to the ground, trying to get their paws over their ears to block out the terrible noise, but they didn't. To my great distress, they continued to run until they came to within a few feet of me, and then stopped, shaking their heads as if an insect were buzzing around them. Then, whining and sinking low to the ground, they slunk down to the far corner of the garden. I heaved a sigh of relief and took my finger off the button. They looked pretty cowed, and I didn't want to cause them any more discomfort than I had to. I ran down to the house and peered through the window.

The pane of glass was thick with grime on both sides. I took a tissue from my pocket, spat to moisten it and made an island of transparency in the muck.

I heard a growl as one of the dogs regained some composure and began to crawl towards me. I gave them another burst.

The inside of the house had never been tidy or clean, but it was now a chaotic jumble, with tables and chairs overturned, cupboards hanging open and flies buzzing here and there in great clouds. I moved to another window and repeated the exercise of creating some visibility. There appeared to be no signs of human life at all, and there seemed to be faeces in clumps on the floor. Then I spotted Rex curled up on one of the armchairs. It seemed that Libby had given him free roam of the house and he had taken full advantage of it. I climbed over the boards and got around the back, which was really only a narrow passage between the rear wall of the house and a tall hedge of brambles and blackthorn. There was no evidence that Libby or Gillian had been there in weeks through these windows either. I made my way to the car and sat in. They weren't home. They hadn't been in a long time.

'Shane?'

'Gillian? Yes, yes, this is me. Where are you? I've been worried sick about you!'

'I'm on the road back from Dublin. Shane, I've had enough of this. I don't want to live this way any more. I'm sick of it. I want you to help me. I'll . . . I'll go back into care. Just come and get me. I'll go wherever you say.'

I couldn't believe it. I had not even started having conversations about care with Gillian. We had never got that far. It seemed that whatever had happened in the couple of months she and Libby had been on the road had prompted Gillian to make the leap all by herself. I silently raised my fist in the air. This was the call I had been waiting for. This was what all the work had been about.

'Gillian, I am really, really pleased. Stay exactly where you are. What's your number there?'

'It's a pay-phone. I can't see any number on it.'

'They're usually on the wall behind the phone, where all the writing and information is. Can you see it?'

'Yeah. Have you a pen?'

When I got off the phone, I just sat back at my desk, grinning from ear to ear. Finally, something had gone right. Josephine came into the office, a sheaf of paper in her hand.

'That review for the Kellys . . . God, what's up with you? You're looking happy for a change. Are you sick or something?'

'Just got a call from Gillian O'Gorman. She's *asked* to be taken into care. I'm about to give Gráinne a ring to organise the bed. Isn't that fucking great?'

Josephine smiled and sat down on the desk opposite me.

'That's really excellent news, Shane. I'm dead chuffed for you. It was a hard case to crack.'

'It was, but now we can put her into a properly

equipped unit and get her the kind of help she really needs. I'm going to make that call.'

'Fair enough. Talk to you later.'

I rang Gráinne Hartigan, who was as pleased as me, and told me to sit tight while she made the necessary arrangements. I got some coffee and was just back at my desk when the phone rang again.

'Shane, bad news I'm afraid. There isn't a single bed available just at the moment. We had a couple of emergency placements last night, and we've actually got children on camp beds in some of the units. She'll have to wait for a bit.'

'She can't wait, Gráinne. You know what this means. This is the opportunity to help this child. I can't ring her back and tell her we've nothing for her! That would be the end of my relationship with her. There would be no coming back. Gráinne, you told me that you could fix this!'

'Well, in all fairness, Shane, it was supposed to be a planned thing, with a little bit of notice. I'm not a magician, as much as everyone would like to think I am. I can't just click my fingers and create a space. I'm sorry.'

'I don't believe it! This is so fucked up.'

'Where is she now?'

'At a pay-phone somewhere between here and Dublin. What am I supposed to tell her, Gráinne?'

'You must tell her to go back to her mother.'

A great chasm opened up inside me, an emptiness that I thought would swallow me whole. I was supposed to be the good guy, the one that showed another path. Now I was pushing her right back into the unhappiness she was trying to flee. How much courage had it taken for her to run from her mother and call me? And I was sending her away.

'Okay, Gráinne. I understand.'

I hung up.

My finger felt like it weighed one hundred pounds as I dialled the number Gillian had given me. Each ring before she answered cut a furrow through my head.

'Shane, it's me.'

'Hey, Gillian.' I heard the lightness in my voice and loathed myself for it. 'Gill, I'm sorry, but there aren't any places available in residential care this evening. Maybe in a day or two. Listen, you need to go back to your mum now, and give me a buzz tomorrow. I swear to you, I will turn the county upside down until I find something for you. I promise you that, and you know I don't break my promises.'

Silence came down the line in a cascade.

'Gillian, please talk to me.'

'Yeah.' Her voice was tiny and young and beaten. 'Yeah, that's okay, Shane. I'll be in touch. I'm sure Mammy will come home soon. She misses the dogs, of course. Bye now.'

Click.

She was gone. I put my head in my hands and clenched my eyes tight shut against bleak reality. I had lost her. There was no use trying to pretend it wasn't so. This was nobody's fault. Gráinne was right

– I hadn't been fair on her – the move *was* supposed to be planned, and it was ridiculous of me to expect that I could just make a call and have Gillian placed within a few hours. But how do you explain economics and cut-backs and management of resources to a frightened child with nowhere to go?

'Shit, shit, shit, shit,' I said, to no one in particular.

I had a cup of tea in my hand, but no stomach for it. Tea, tea, tea. Everywhere I went, people expected me to drink tea. I wrapped my coat more tightly around myself. It wasn't my leather one, but a long, grey overcoat, not unlike a trenchoat. It was comforting. I hadn't taken it off in a few days, and found that it made me feel a lot better to have it on. Kind of cocooned.

Cocoon. Wasn't that a movie? That guy from the *Police Academy* films had been in it. Steve Guttenburgh, that was him. His career had sunk without a trace, hadn't it? That movie had been about old people. You don't see too many movies about old people, at least none that don't have Walter Matthau in them. Walter Matthau was a good actor. Was. Had he died? I couldn't remember.

'Shane, wouldn't you think that the McCoys would love it here?'

'What?'

I was sitting in the kitchen of an old farmhouse in the early afternoon. Zara, a fostering social worker, was with me. She thought that she had identified a family for the McCoys. A couple in late middle age sat before us, looking at me with a mix of concern and impatience. Having been built up as the main worker on the case, someone with a deep insight into these children, I had proceeded to contribute absolutely nothing to the conversation and to very obviously drift. I was finding it difficult to sustain my concentration for any length of time.

'I'm sorry. Yes, yes I think they could be very happy here. You have a lovely home.' I addressed the couple, Jim and Harriet Kenneally. 'Are you quite certain that you don't mind taking *three* children? It's a huge undertaking, and they've been through an extremely traumatic time. It won't all be plain sailing. There will be resistance, from all of them.'

'We had four of our own, Mr Dunphy,' Harriet said. 'They've grown up and moved on. They come home of course, to visit, but they're dispersed across the globe and we're knocking around in this big house. I miss the sound of children. I think that we can give a good home to these kids.'

Zara nodded and scribbled something down in her notebook.

'There will be a fostering course. You'll be able to facilitate me in doing that with you?'

'Oh, certainly,' said Jim.

'Then the Fostering Panel will have to meet to agree the placement. This is by no means definite.'

'We understand. Every precaution must be taken to ensure they're right for us, and we for them.'

'I'll arrange for a visit next week,' Zara continued. 'Let's see how you all get along together.'

'We'll look forward to it.'

I stood with Zara at the cars in the broad cobbled yard. A verdant field spread before us as far as either of us could see. Four beautiful horses gambolled there. I knew that there were more behind the great house in stables and other pastures the family owned.

'What d'you think?'

'I think they're a gift. But they've got their work cut out for them. The children have all fallen back on old patterns of behaviour. Cordelia is playing the mother and I'm damned if I can get through to her. Victor's just turned right in on himself again, and Ibar might as well be on some other planet. It's a hell of a lot to put on those two old dears.'

'Don't underestimate them, Shane. They've hidden depths, I think. And look at this place. I wish they'd foster me!'

'All we can do is hope it works out. How long will the course take?'

'Well, I'm pulling out the stops here. I should have it done in six weeks. They're prepared to work quickly.'

'Let me know how it goes. God knows, the McCoys are due a break.'

'Aren't we all!'

'Yes. We certainly are.'

12

'And will either of them make official statements? Will this Mrs Jones speak to the police?'

'No.'

'Do you have any new evidence at all beyond this interview and disclosure?'

'No.'

'No addresses of places the children were taken to? Dates? Names of alleged abusers?'

'No.'

Josephine had her back to me, looking out the window of her office. When she spoke it was in muted tones. She didn't like what she had to tell me any more than I did.

'Connie was put into care before because of confirmed evidence of sexual abuse. *Physical evidence.* She did not wish to remain there. After this two-week absence you've latched on to, another medical examination *was* performed. There was no sign of her having had sexual intercourse, no bruising, no traces of semen. It doesn't add up. And there are small inconsistencies in the stories. Little things, but they're there nonetheless. I'm not sure what you want us to do with this.'

'I'm not sure either. She's telling the truth. I know she's telling the truth.'

'She may well be. But there's a Supervision Order on the child. The parents and Mick are subject to a good deal of psychiatric intervention. Beyond that, I don't see that I can do much more. I wish I could be more positive.'

'So do I.'

'Shane, everyone who has ever worked on the case has known that there was unbelievable deprivation and abuse going on in that family. It has been an accepted fact for decades. But you're a professional – you know the score. We *cannot* plough in there with accusations and presumptions and half-arsed stories from an old woman, no matter how sensational and frightening they are. I'm sorry, Shane. We just can't.'

'I know.'

She turned and there was concern on her face.

'You're due some leave. Take it. You're going to collapse if you don't.'

'Yeah, I will. There are just a few things I need to wind up. A few loose ends, y'know?'

'If you don't give me a list of days you're taking within the next week, I'll give them to you myself. You're going to be a liability if you don't sort yourself out.'

'Point taken.'

'How are things going with the McCoys?'

'Good, I think. They've been visiting the Kenneallys a couple of times a week. Zara has been supervising. She tells me that there's a kind of . . . *tentative* bonding going on. Ibar thinks he's died and gone to heaven out on the farm. Victor seems to have come out of himself a bit. Jim has a nice way about him. He's safe, y'know. Gentle. Doesn't drink, doesn't smoke. He's firm but quietly so. Victor responds to that. He's been craving a male role-model that he can feel secure with. And Cordelia – we'll see. She seems to have reserved judgement, for the moment. Harriet is spending a lot of time with her . . . more than that, I can't say. Cordy is keeping her own counsel. All she'll tell me is that she thinks they're very nice. Not much of an analysis, but that's as much as she'll give.'

'Ah, you can't rush these things,' Josephine said. 'We've kind of pushed the two families together. They're doing remarkably well, under the circumstances.'

'I suppose they are.'

'Keep me informed.'

'Will do.'

I lit a cigarette and watched as Geraldine Kelly left the Post Office pushing baby Christine in her pram. It was the day the Children's Allowance was collected, so I knew she'd be there. I let her get one hundred yards or so down the street and then followed. A light rain had started to fall and she was hurrying to get into the shelter of a nearby shopping centre, so I broke into a brisk jog. I reached her just as she was wrestling to get the pram through the doorway of the complex.

'Let me give you a hand with that.'

'Thanks very much – oh. It's you.'

She glowered, but accepted my assistance. I held the heavy door for her and she pushed the buggy through.

'I'll be seein' you,' she said, moving away as soon as she was inside.

'Hold on a minute. Can I buy you a cup of coffee or something?'

She stopped and looked at me, agog.

'Are you comin' on to me?'

'No! No, it's not like that. I need to talk to you. Just let me buy you a cup of tea and a bun and listen to what I have to say. Ten minutes.'

'I don't know. You're kind of an eejit.'

'Look, there's a café over there. Just a few minutes, that's all I ask.'

Begrudgingly she followed me to the coffee shop. The term 'coffee' appeared to have been applied in its loosest possible definition, because what arrived in my cup bore almost no resemblance to the beverage I had ordered. I pushed it aside.

'So what do you want?' Geraldine asked me around a mouthful of cream doughnut.

'I think we can help each other. And by helping each other we can help little Christine there' – the baby was asleep in her pram – 'and Connie.'

'What are you goin' on about?'

'What would you say if I told you that I had a flat organised for you to move into with Christine?'

'I can't afford to move into a flat!'

'I have spoken to Social Welfare about rent allowance, and I can go through any other entitlements you may be due. You'll be well able to afford it.'

'But . . . but I don't want to move anywhere.'

I sighed and rubbed my eyes. Why was it never easy? Could it not just go smoothly, just the once? I hadn't wanted to bring out the big guns, but she was giving me no choice.

'I know about Mick. And the "visitors".'

She stopped chewing, and for a moment she turned such a violent shade of green, I thought she would be sick. 'Don't know what you're talkin' about. You're just bullshittin' me.'

'You don't need to say anything, Geraldine. Just listen to me. It doesn't happen to you any more, because you're too old. They don't like women, just children. Denise is safe from it too, she's just the wrong side of adolescence for them. But Connie, she's still mostly a kid. And Christine . . . well, she's a baby. When did it start for you, Geraldine? When did they come for you first? I'd guess that Christine sleeps in the same room as you, yeah?'

She nodded.

'The night will come when you'll wake up and they'll be taking her. Will you be able to protect her? Will you be able to fight them off?'

She had turned as white as a ghost and tears welled

274

in her eyes. The doughnut, half-eaten, dropped to the tabletop.

'You shouldn't say stuff like that to me. You've no right.'

'It's true. You've thought it too, if you're honest with yourself. I'm showing you a way out. I know it's scary, but there will be people to help you and you will be safe. I just want you to do one thing for me.'

'What?'

'Take Connie with you.'

'Connie?'

'I want her to be safe too. You can help each other out. She needs someone to look after her. She's still a kid. You'll need help with Christine, and well, it's easier with two, isn't it?'

She used the paper napkin to dab her eyes.

'What d'you think?' I asked.

'When can I see the flat?'

'Right now.'

'All right. Show me, then.'

The flat had two bedrooms and was fully furnished and newly decorated. Marjorie, the Family Support Worker, had agreed to work with the girls intensively over the initial period, and to keep an eye on them for as long as necessary after that. Geraldine agreed that her parents and Mick should know nothing about the move until the day arrived. They had huge potential for creating mayhem, and I wanted the transition to be as stress-free as possible.

I wasn't innocent enough to believe that they would be completely safe, but they were saf*er*. There was a buzzer and intercom system, they were on the third floor – they were as secure as it was possible to make them. The real danger was that they would actually let Mick and a gang of strange men in. That may sound unlikely, but the psychological stranglehold the abuser has over the victim is preternaturally strong, and never to be underestimated. I could only trust in their desire to protect Christine, and in the fact that, with Mrs Jones's help, Connie had already made a move away from her home and its horrors. Marjorie would also work with them on developing ways of avoiding falling back into old, dangerous patterns of behaviour. I simply had to believe in them. They *could* do it. It was time to let go.

They brought clothes, soft toys, Connie's schoolbooks and that was all. Marjorie and I had stocked up the kitchen with food, any cooking utensils that were absent and bought some fresh flowers as a house-warming gift. I left Marjorie in the flat with Geraldine and the baby, and Connie walked me down to my car. She had been quiet throughout the whole process of the move. She had seemed neither elated nor frightened when I told her about my and Geraldine's plan (Geraldine and I had decided to tell her we had come up with the idea together), and had gone about her business quietly and calmly, never mentioning it to either of us until that morning, when she had come out to the car with her bags packed and ready to go, a determined look on her face. As we walked to the car she was subdued and thoughtful, chewing her lower lip and lagging behind. I opened the driver's door and turned to her. I reckoned that she wanted to get the goodbye over with as quickly as possible, so I determined not to prolong it for her. I extended my hand and we shook.

'Well, that's that. Marjorie will be visiting you every day for the next while, until you're properly settled in. I'll pop in and out, make sure you're okay, but we won't be seeing each other as much as we have been. You know you can call me if you need anything.'

She still said nothing, looking at me from under her eyes. I patted her on the shoulder.

'I'd better be going,' I said, moving to sit in.

'Shane,' she suddenly said, and grabbed me in a fierce hug.

I almost jumped. She had never made any attempt to touch me before. I put my arms around her and hugged her back.

'Thank you,' she whispered. 'Thank you for believing me. Thank you for helping us.'

She held me for a while longer, then turned and without a word ran back into the building. I watched her through a haze of unexpected tears and started the engine, anxious for the monotonous anonymity of the road.

*

They took me off the O'Gorman case.

I didn't want to leave it, not in its state of desperate confusion and lack of resolution. But Gillian didn't want to see me or speak to me, and it seemed that the case would lapse back into the fugue state it had been in before I had been appointed.

It gnawed at me. Another worker had been sent out to try to re-establish some links between the department and the family, but to no avail. As I had suspected, the rejection that day, when Gillian had actually *asked* for help, had been too much. I had let her down, despite the fact that I had always told her I would not. I had done what everyone else in her life had done. It sickened me to think that I had been instrumental in killing any last vestiges of trust and confidence in this child.

I would not abandon Gillian without one last try. We had a year behind us – much of it good. I just hoped that this would stand me in good stead, that somewhere in among the hurt and damage was a sense that, even if I could not always deliver, I had her best interests at heart and would not purposely set out to hurt her.

I don't remember the drive out to her house, but I know it was mid-afternoon when I got there. I grabbed the dog-deterrent from the back seat and had the button pressed before I opened the door. I didn't even look at where the animals were. I felt a sense of urgency for some reason, a deep-rooted need to see her, to know she was all right. I knocked loudly on the door. There was no answer; I hadn't expected one. I walked to the nearest window and peered through. I could dimly see a shape curled up on the beaten up old couch. Was it she?

I knocked loudly on the glass. There was no movement. I abandoned all semblance of cleanliness and used the sleeve of my beloved coat to clear some of the gunk so I could see more clearly. It was Gillian. I banged again, louder this time. Then I noticed something: a stain of red on the arm of the couch upon which she lay. I squinted to get a better look. There seemed to be some of it on the carpet also, and I thought I could see more on the wall nearby. Fear gripped me, and I ran to the door, using the machine to smash the glass panel so I could get my arm through to reach the handle. Then I was in and it was so much worse than I had thought.

A Stanley knife lay on the floor among the blood that had seeped there. She had cut deep grooves into her flesh, all down both arms. She seemed to be catatonic or semi-conscious from loss of blood – the air was rich with its coppery stench, the cushions upon which she was sprawled were sodden with it, and she was deathly pale. I frantically called for the emergency services and used some tea-towels, the only bindings I could find, to bandage her wounds. Then I held her, rocking her in my arms and talking to her, telling her that it was okay, I was here now, she would be all right. Time became a crazy drip, drip, drip. All that was real was me and the girl.

I seemed to drift in and out of awareness with her.

I heard voices and the ambulance crew were there. I answered their questions and let them take her from me, watched as they did their work with sure hands and a calmness that I could not feel.

'She'll be fine, Mr Dunphy,' one of them told me. 'She's lost a lot of blood, but the cuts were mostly superficial. You called us just in time.'

She was put on a trolley and brought to the ambulance. As they were lifting her in, she snapped into consciousness, eyes wide open. I saw her start to panic. She did not know what was happening. She was tied down to stop her falling from the stretcher, and a drip had been attached to her arm.

'Gillian, it's okay, it's me, Shane. We're just taking you over to the hospital. You hurt yourself.'

'Shane?'

'Yes, honey. I'm here.'

I came up beside her and she seemed to relax for a moment, but only a moment. Anger built to rage so quickly, it seemed almost as if she were becoming a different person before my eyes.

'You left me! *You left me!* You said you wouldn't and you did. They sent someone else out, and she said she would be my new worker. You want to leave me too! Why don't you like me any more? Why?'

She struggled and shouted, trying to get free, her anger and fear giving her strength even in her weakened state. I tried to hush her without success. My presence only seemed to be making her more agitated. One of the medics gave her a shot and she sagged again. The last thing I saw in her eyes was that terrible accusation: *how could you have done this to me*?

We brought her to the hospital. I waited while they worked on her, drinking the disgusting coffee from the vending machine and standing outside to smoke. When they allowed me in to see her, she was so doped up she didn't know who I was, which was probably a good thing. Libby was uncontactable.

I sat by her bedside in one of the uncomfortable hospital chairs. She mumbled every now and again in her drug-fuelled haze, but I could not understand what she was saying. Sometime during the night I dozed off.

I don't know what woke me.

For a second I had no idea where I was or why I had an awful crick in my neck. I sat up with a start, massaging the screaming muscles of my shoulders.

'Bastard.'

The word was hissed from the bed beside me. The curtains had been drawn around us, and the rest of the ward was in dimness.

'Hi, Gillian. How are you feeling?'

'Bastard!'

The word was spoken more loudly this time. I shushed her and moved over closer.

'C'mon, I know you're mad with me, but listen, *I don't want to leave you*. You misunderstood. They sent someone else out because you said you didn't want to see me. That's all.'

'*Bastard!*'

She screamed at me now and tried to grab me, her nails bared and such hatred on her face that I knew she was truly lost to me. I held her down as she thrashed and called for a nurse. I held my head back as her teeth clicked. She struck like a snake, trying to bite my face. She kicked and spat, and I saw a red stain spreading across her bandages as her stitches burst. Two nurses pushed through the drapes and a hypodermic needle glinted. All became quiet again.

'I think you should leave her, Mr Dunphy,' the nurse told me firmly. 'You are only aggravating the child. I'm sorry, but I'd like you to go.'

I nodded. She was right. Josephine had been, too. I was a liability. I drove home, took some headed paper from my writing desk, and composed a letter of resignation.

'You're sure about this?'

'Yes. Certain. I can't do it any more. I'm sorry.'

Josephine was holding my letter. It didn't say much. She had read it in about fifteen seconds. She didn't look surprised.

'No apology necessary. Just as long as you're sure. I'm glad you can see it's not working out for you.'

'Any word on Gillian?'

'She's in restraints. They're going to move her to the psychiatric hospital as soon as it's safe to do so. She's had a complete breakdown.'

'What's the prognosis?'

'They have no idea, at the moment. She's not speaking, at least not in any language they can understand. She seems to have reverted to some kind of feral state. I'm guessing she'll be insitutionalised, for a while, at least. I know you blame yourself for this, and I'm not even going to get into that with you. If blame has to be apportioned, then point your finger at the system. Everyone wanted to do their best for her. She fell through the cracks. It happens. It's unfortunate, but what can I say? Maybe she's where she needs to be. Have you thought of that?'

'I'm tired of thinking. My brain hurts. I'll work out my notice.'

'I know you will. What are you going to do?'

'I don't know. Something different. For a while anyway.'

'You won't be able to stay away for long. This is what you do, Shane. You'll come back to it, sooner or later.'

Betty and I picked up the McCoys from Dympna's. There were tears and hugs and kisses, and then we were on the road, headed for the Kenneallys. The visits had gone extremely well, and Jim and Harriet had applied themselves with great enthusiasm to the fostering course. The Fostering Panel, a group of social workers, doctors, psychologists and administrators whose job it was to approve each foster placement, had met and looked at all the factors, and decided that we should proceed.

I drove. Betty's car was already at the Kenneallys. Once I had left the McCoys in their new home, I would return to the office and clear out my desk. It was my last job on my last day. I didn't know how I felt, or how I *should* feel. I looked at the children in the rear-view mirror. They seemed to be going through the same emotional turmoil as me.

'How are you doing in the back?'

'Fine.'

'You sure?' Betty asked.

'Well, I'm a little scared,' Victor offered slowly, looking sideways at his sister. She shot him a glance but did not try to quiet him.

'Horsies!' Ibar said happily. 'Gonna ride de horsies! Clip clop! Clip clop!'

'That's right, kiddo,' I said, laughing.

'They seem really nice,' Cordelia said. 'It's just, well, they're not Mum and Dad, you know? They're just some old couple we don't even know. What if it doesn't work out? What if we find out in six months' time that they're psychos or something?'

'Well, if that does happen, which I very much doubt, there's nothing written in stone that says you have to stay,' Betty told them. 'Of course, you could always go into this with a really positive attitude and just tell yourself that it's going to be great.'

'Yeah, right!' Cordelia snorted and went back to looking at the landscape as it sailed past her window.

Jim and Harriet were waiting at the door when we parked in their beautiful yard. The windows were all bedecked with flowers and the smell of freshly baking bread wafted out of the kitchen. They greeted the children with smiles and Ibar ran straight to Harriet and jumped into her arms.

'Hello, little man,' she said, grinning in delight.

'Harry, Harry,' he called, hugging her around the neck.

Victor stood uncertainly to the side, but Jim went over and took his hand, shaking it gently.

'Welcome, Victor.' He looked over at Cordelia. 'I'd like to show you your rooms. Now, there's one we've done up with three beds in, if you'd like to all stay together this evening, seeing as it's your first night. Or we have three separate rooms. You can decide. Once you're here a bit and are sure you like it, we can talk about how you'd like them decorated and whatnot. They're your rooms, so it's fine with us, whatever you'd like.'

Victor could not suppress a smile. Cordelia was still very non-committal, but I could tell that this simple show of sensitivity had made a big impression on her.

'You go on ahead,' I told them. 'We'll start bringing your stuff in.'

Like Connie and Geraldine, the McCoy's worldly possessions did not amount to much, and it did not take Betty and me long to bring their bags from the car and lug them up the wide staircase to the communal bedroom they had decided to sleep in that night, although Victor had already claimed a sunlit room to the rear of the house, overlooking a wooded area, as his own. He would move in next week, he told Jim solemnly. Jim nodded, patted him on the back and told him to do it in his own good time. The room would be there next week, or next year, for that matter.

I found Cordelia sitting outside on the fence, looking at the horses in the pasture. One had come over and was nuzzling her hand.

'They're lovely, aren't they?' she asked.

'Yeah. There's something so . . . I don't know . . . regal about horses.'

'I meant Jim and Harriet.'

'Oh. Yes, I think they're really, really decent people. And I think that they're going to pull out all the stops to make this work.'

'I think so too.'

'But? C'mon, I know there's a "but" coming.'

She laughed and leant her head on my shoulder.

'You're going away, aren't you?'

'Yeah. I'll keep tabs on you for a bit. But you're kind of under Zara's jurisdiction now, and anyway, you don't need me hanging around any more. I just know that this is going to work out fine for you.'

'I don't think I'm going to be able to call them Mum and Dad. Not ever.'

'They don't expect you to. They know where you're coming from.'

'Ibar probably will, though, won't he? He'll forget Dad. He's so little.'

'You and Victor can be his memories. You can keep your dad alive in all the things we talked about. The good stuff. The fun things you did together, the happy times. Tell him about those, and he'll remember them.'

'Yeah. We'll do that.'

'Why don't you go in with the others? They're about to have their tea, I think.'

'Stay out here with me for a while, will you, Shane? Let's just sit quietly together, like this. Do you mind?'

'No. I don't mind at all.'

'Thanks. Thanks for . . . well, you know.'

'I know. You're welcome, sweetheart.'

And we sat together in the early evening as the sounds of a new family being born spilled out of the doorway of the house and warmed us both.

Acknowledgements

Thanks are due to many who contributed to the writing and publication of this book:

I wish to particularly express gratitude to Jonathan Williams, my agent, who was the first to read most of the text and whose editing skills were invaluable.

Alison Walsh was the first person to express confidence in the work being publishable. Thank you, Alison, for your kindness, friendship and boundless good humour. All the staff at Gill & Macmillan were incredibly enthusiastic and supportive. Thank you all.

John Connolly is a hero who became a friend. John's patience, advice and selfless generosity helped me through a particularly difficult period in the writing. I will always be grateful, John.

Dr Arthur Williamson has been a friend and mentor to me for several years now. His guidance was instrumental in the completion of this book. As always, Arthur, thank you.

Deirdre, my wife, was the first person to read *Wednesday's Child* from start to finish, and her comments on style, content and technical details were much appreciated.

I wish to thank all the children and co-workers whom I encountered during my career in social care.

This book is dedicated to all of you. There was not a single person among you from whom I did not learn something, about life and about myself. Thank you.